Introduction to
Quality Control

Introduction to Quality Control

ARCHIBALD JAMIESON

Niagara College of Applied
Arts and Technology

Reston Publishing Company, Inc.

A Prentice-Hall Company
Reston, Virginia

Library of Congress Cataloging in Publication Data

Jamieson, Archibald.
  Introduction to quality control.

  Includes index.
  1. Quality control. I. Title.
TS156.J324   620'.0045   81–13877
ISBN 0–8359–3264–8   AACR2

Editorial/production supervision and
interior design by Norma M. Karlin
Cover photo by Fraser Jamieson,
Mississauga, Ontario
Manufacturing buyer: Ron Chapman

10   9   8   7   6   5   4   3   2

Printed in the United States of America

Contents

v

Preface

This book has been written for two distinctly different groups of readers. The first group consists of College of Applied Arts and Technology (or Community College) students who are specializing in Industrial Management, Manufacturing Technology, or Industrial Engineering Technology and who require a text on the introductory theory and practice of quality control. The second group consists of managers, engineers, technologists and others already in industry who find themselves with large amounts of information on product or process quality characteristics and feel the need for a systematic approach to the analysis of this material, but are not sure where to start. It may be a long time since school days and they may want a book that will review the basics without complicating the issue with unnecessary theory.

Nevertheless, the subject matter of this text necessitates some understanding of a few statistical principles, and no attempt has been made to avoid this issue. In fact, theory and practice are interwoven throughout the book. Only the principles that relate to quality-control practices are dealt with, however, so it is not necessary to have studied "statistics" as a prerequisite subject prior to the use of this book. Also, the theory is limited to only that which is necessary for an understanding of the practices described. Advanced statistical analysis theory has been avoided.

It has been the author's observation that industry abounds with cases where quality-control programs have been short-lived because either someone studied the theory behind statistical quality control, but put charts together that no one would look at, or someone studied only the practical procedures for the preparation of charts, but failed miserably to understand their significance. It is hoped that this text will help the reader to avoid these pitfalls by intermingling theory and practice, rather than separating them into individual compartments.

Many excellent textbooks on quality control go into great detail about the analysis of results, but in this text we will concentrate on understanding the appropriateness of the various types of controls and will confine analysis to only that which is necessary for the establishment of rational control limits. The objective will be to present enough material to enable the student to set up appropriate control procedures upon completion of his or her studies.

After experience has been gained in the application of the material contained in this book, the "student" may go on to more advanced texts on the subject and thus gain even more benefits from the practices that have been established.

Introduction to
Quality Control

Introduction

1-1 IF THEY CAN MAKE SOME THE RIGHT SIZE, WHY CAN'T THEY MAKE THEM ALL THE RIGHT SIZE?

The supervisor or manager with a background in almost any aspect of manufacturing has learned to expect variation in results and, to some extent, to accept them as an unfortunate fact of industrial life. However, the road to management can be by a variety of routes, and not all these routes teach a person to expect results to vary when the same procedures are apparently followed.

It is the latter group which ask such exasperating questions as, "If they can make some the right size, why can't they make them all the right size?" or, when corrections are necessary, "Why can't they make them right in the first place?" These types of questions are exasperating to manufacturing supervisors, but they are not stupid questions. They exasperate the manufacturer often because he or she has accepted the situation, but has no reasonable answers to the questions.

This text should provide some of the answers and also show how variation can be kept under control.

1

1-2   ATTRIBUTES AND VARIABLES

One of the most difficult words to define is "quality," but we all have some kind of mental image of what it means to us for some particular item. It may be the fine surface finish on a machined item or the smooth movement of a mechanical device, or perhaps it is the lack of defects on an enameled surface.

In general, however, we divide quality-control procedures into two types: (1) the control of variables and (2) the control of attributes. A variable is any characteristic of a product or item which can be measured on a continuous scale, and an attribute is a characteristic which is either possessed or not possessed by an item. The diameter of a shaft, the carbon content of steel, the tensile strength of brass are all variables. Acceptable or reject products, undersize, on size, oversize products, or the number of pin holes on a polished surface are all attributes. Variables are measured on a continuous scale and may, therefore, have fractional values, whereas attributes are always discrete whole numbers.

Attribute control is generally after-the-fact control; that is, the product reaches a certain stage in manufacture and is then classified, for example, as being either acceptable or unacceptable. Variable control, however, may be after-the-fact or before-the-fact, as it is sometimes possible to measure a variable and to change its value while a process continues to run.

The statistical principles involved in the analysis of whole numbers are not necessarily the same as those involved with continuous measurement, and, so as not to introduce too much theory at the outset, the theory of variables will be presented immediately before the chapters on the control of variables and the theory of whole numbers immediately before the material on attribute control.

1-3   VARIATION AS A MEASURE OF QUALITY

We have said that "quality" is a difficult word to define and, at least as far as industry is concerned, there is no absolute definition that will satisfy all conditions. A Rolls Royce automobile has quality, but so also has a Ford. In fact, the quality of the Ford is such that more people will be prepared to buy that level of quality than will buy the quality of a Rolls Royce. So the level of quality which is acceptable in an industrial product is related not only to what is possible, but also to the economic circumstances surrounding the manufacture and sale of the product.

We cannot measure two different products in units of quality and compare them on an absolute scale. This is just not possible; no such scale exists. What then can we do? We can measure the amount of variation which occurs in some characteristic of the products.

If variation is a fact of life in manufacturing, and if the objects of our study are characteristics which are measured on a continuous scale, then the amount and nature of this variation can be the means whereby we control the consistency of the product. When we set out to manufacture a number of items having a characteristic of a given dimension (e.g., a shaft of 2.000-in. diameter or a steel with a 0.30% carbon content), we know that not all the items (or material) produced will have the aimed-at dimension. Some will be a little below, and some a little above the aimed-at value. If we now compare the amount of this variation (from the minimum to the maximum value) for different products and for different processes, we find that there does not appear to be any consistency in the amount of this variation.

Not only does the amount of this variation differ from product to product, and from process to process, but with some of the items we may occasionally find results that are so far away from the aimed-at value that we cannot avoid the conclusion that something appears to be out of control.

Here then is how we will attempt to measure and control the quality of a variable: we will try to determine the "normal" amount of variation from the aimed-at value, and we will try to identify the causes of unusually large variations which appear to indicate that something out of the ordinary is happening.

1-4 QUALITY CHARACTERISTICS

The term "characteristic" has already been used in relation to a variable which has been studied. In quality control work we use the term *quality characteristic* to mean any property of a product which can be used as a measure of the quality of the product. It may be a dimension such as the thickness, width, or length of an item. It may be an "element" in the composition of a material, such as the zinc content of brass, the butterfat content of milk, or the sugar content of wine. It may be a property such as the tensile strength of steel, the electrical resistivity of a conductor, or the density of compacted granular material. These are only a few of the quality characteristics which may be used as a measure of the quality of an item.

Each industry and each particular product has its own set of quality characteristics which may be used as the means of control, but not all characteristics which are generated by a process will necessarily be the subject of control procedures.

When a product is manufactured, a number of characteristics are often generated simultaneously. For example, the machining of a spindle will generate a diameter, a length, a surface finish, and a degree of straightness. The manufacture of cast iron will generate a carbon content, but also silicon, manganese, and sulfur contents (to name only four).

Quality-control programs do not necessarily attempt to measure every possible characteristic, but only those which are critical to the development of the required properties in the product.

1-5   SOURCES OF VARIATION

Variation which occurs about an aimed-at value has four recognized sources.

1-5.1   The Raw Material

What constitutes raw material differs in different industries. Iron ore is the raw material to the steelmaker and steel the finished product, but steel is the raw material for the shipbuilder, the car manufacturer, and many others. It makes no difference which phase of manufacturing you are engaged in, the material you use as raw material comes to you from a natural or a manufacturing system having its own inherent degree of variation. These variations in the quality characteristics of the raw material are with you before your processes even begin to change the nature of your raw material.

1-5.2   The Operator

When an operation or process is started or stopped by an operator at some specific stage, and human judgment or visual measurement are used to determine when this stage has been reached, then variations will occur. This variation itself will vary depending upon the skill of the operator, the time of day, the mental attitude of the operator, and his or her physical condition.

1-5.3   The Process

The process may consist of a melting furnace, a lathe, a series of screens, a mixer, a grinder, a rolling mill, a loom, or any of the other countless means of processing which exist today, but they all have some things in common. They have all been already manufactured by some other series of processes and, therefore, contain the variations inherent in the raw materials and operator performance in these previous processes. Even a piece of "precision" equipment has been made to some *tolerance*, or acceptable amount of variation, especially where two or more parts fit together.

1-5.4   The Method of Measuring the Variable

If we measured off some lengths of wood to the nearest tenth of an inch, they might all appear to be dead to size, but if we then measured them to the nearest hundredth of an inch, we would discover that a considerable amount of variation exists in the lengths of the various pieces. Similarly, if we machined to the nearest hundredth of an inch and then measured to the nearest thousandth of an inch, we would discover variations in the size of parts we had previously considered to be identical. What this means is that the more precise the method of measurement, the greater the amount of variation discovered in the quality characteristic. Also, the measuring device must be maintained in top quality and be regularly checked against some standard. Failure to do this can result in the apparent occurrence of variations which do not in fact exist.

It is important for all those charged with responsibility for product quality to be aware of the four preceding sources of variation. An unacceptable level of variation in the end product could be due to deficiencies at one or more of the sources of variation. An attempt to reduce costs by purchasing a lower-priced raw material might, for example, introduce a greater amount of variation, which cannot be compensated for by either the operator or the process. The end result can be an increase in rejects and an overall increase rather than decrease in costs.

The purchase of new equipment can sometimes be justified on the basis of quality improvements. If a quality-control program can show that the major source of variation is an old run-down piece of equipment, and if an equipment manufacturer can prove or guarantee the range of capability of a new machine, then it should be possible to pay for the new machine from savings resulting from reductions in rejects generated by the older equipment.

1-6   CLASSIFICATION OF QUALITY

A further complication about the quality of an industrial product is that a particular quality level may occur by intent or by chance, and we, therefore, break down quality into a number of classifications.

1-6.1   Quality of Design

This is the level of quality which the designer or engineer intended the product to have. It is generally expressed in terms of the maximum amount of tolerable variation which may exist in the end product and is known as the *tolerance* or *tolerance specification.*

For example, suppose we have two items, each with the same aimed-at dimension or *nominal size,* but the tolerance is greater for one of the items:

> **Item 1.   Nominal size = 0.800 in.**
> **Tolerance = ±0.002 in.***
> **Item 2.   Nominal size = 0.800 in.**
> **Tolerance = ±0.004 in.**

Item 1 is said to have a higher quality of design than item 2.

If a tolerance is quoted as a number without being prefixed by the ± symbols, this implies that the figures quoted are for the total tolerance spread. For example, a tolerance of ±0.002 in. is the same as a tolerance of 0.004 in., and a tolerance of ±0.004 in. is the same as a tolerance of 0.008 in.

A question often asked in manufacturing is, "Why is the specification so tight?; if they would only widen the tolerance we would not have to reject so much of our product." So what is the criterion for establishing the quality of design? It is, or should be, the in-

---

* The symbols ± are read "plus or minus" and indicate a range in size for item 1 of from 0.798 in. to 0.802 in. and for item 2 of from 0.796 in. to 0.804 in.

service performance requirements of the end product. Closer tolerances entail higher manufacturing costs, so where there is the possibility of wide latitude in the final dimension, composition, or property, the designer should give careful thought to matching the tolerance with the capability of the particular process being used. Any tolerance which is based only on someone's idealistic concept of what "ought" to be should be viewed with suspicion.

It is important to emphasize here that in quality-control work the word "design" is not restricted to a two-dimensional drawing or plan. It includes any aimed-at chemical or physical specification which has been determined in advance to be the quality objective.

1-6.2   Quality of Conformance to Design

It is one thing for someone to specify the tolerance which has to be met and another thing to have to meet that tolerance. The closer a manufacturer or process comes to the aimed-at value, the higher is the quality of conformance. For example, if two machines are producing a part to the same nominal size, but machine 1 produces to a range of ± 0.003 in., while machine 2 produces to a range of ± 0.004 in., then we say that machine 1 has a higher quality of conformance.

Even if the quality of conformance is such that results occasionally fall outside the specification limits, the inspection or sampling procedures should be such that there is only a very low probability of any of this off-specification material reaching the customer. In other words, what the customer actually receives should conform closely to the quality of design, but the manufacturing costs in the plant will be tied in closely to the quality of conformance.

The whole field of quality of conformance to design is of particular importance to the student of statistical quality control, for it is in the recording and analysis of results in this area that most of our work is concentrated.

1-6.3   Quality of Performance

This is perhaps the thing which most of us have in mind when we speak about the quality of an automobile, a television set, paint, ice cream, or any of the many items on which we pass judgment. Quality of performance is basically the ability of the product to perform its technical function in a satisfactory manner at an economically acceptable cost. We expect a lawnmower to be able to cut grass and to be maneuverable; we expect an electric shaver to give a close shave and to do it in a relatively short time; we expect paint to retain its color and texture and to adhere to a surface for a long period of time; and we expect all these things at a competitive market price.

Quality of performance, then, is linked to both economics and to technical performance and, in a competitive society, is monitored closely by the customer. An effective sales department in a producing company will, therefore, not only sell the product, but will feed back to the design department any comments on quality of performance.

In an effectively run company, therefore, each of the three classifications of quality will interact with one another. Information on quality of performance may cause quality of design to be either tightened or loosened, and this in turn will influence the ease with which the manufacturing department will conform to the design.

1-7   TOLERANCE SPECIFICATION AND PROCESS COSTS

It has already been mentioned that closer tolerances entail higher manufacturing costs, and it is important that we look at this in more detail. If the reader has ever cut lumber for the upright slats on a fence, such as a picket fence, you have probably marked off each length with a pencil and then cut with a saw, and it has not mattered if you cut on the line or to the left or right of the line. There might be more than $\frac{1}{8}$ in. of difference between some of the slats, but they perform their technical requirement and take a minimum of time to produce. However, if the upright slats were to fit between top and bottom horizontal boards, and if you wanted them to fit tightly, you may have to plane or sand the ends of some of the pieces to get them to fit.

In the second case you have worked to a closer tolerance and it has obviously taken more working time to do so. It is the same in manufacturing. Whether it is a refining process, a mixing operation, or metal cutting, the closer the limits within which you must finish, the higher the cost of operating the process. This cost may be due to increased time or skill or to the need to include in the process costs the writing off of more expensive equipment.

In *Quality Control: Theory and Applications* by Bertrand L. Hansen (Prentice-Hall, Inc., Englewood Cliffs, New Jersey), figures are quoted from the Ordnance Management Engineering Training Agency for the relative costs of various machine-shop processes (see Table 1-1). Taking an example from this table for an operation such

Table 1-1   PROPORTIONATE COST OF OBTAINING VARIOUS TOLERANCES[a]

Range of Sizes		Total Tolerances (In.)								
From	To and Incl.	0.0002	0.00025	0.0004	0.0005	0.0008	0.0012	0.002	0.003	0.005
0.000	0.599	0.0002	0.00025	0.0004	0.0005	0.0008	0.0012	0.002	0.003	0.005
0.600	0.999	0.00025	0.0003	0.00045	0.0006	0.001	0.0015	0.0025	0.004	0.006
1.000	1.499	0.0003	0.0004	0.0005	0.0008	0.0012	0.002	0.003	0.005	0.008
1.500	2.799	0.0004	0.0005	0.0006	0.001	0.0015	0.0025	0.004	0.006	0.010
2.800	4.499	0.0005	0.0006	0.0008	0.0012	0.002	0.003	0.005	0.008	
4.500	7.799	0.0006	0.0007	0.001	0.0015	0.0025	0.004	0.006	0.010	
7.800	13.599	0.0007	0.0008	0.0012	0.002	0.003	0.005	0.008	0.012	
13.600	20.999	0.0008	0.001	0.0015	0.0025	0.004	0.006	0.010	0.015	
21.00 and over*										
Lapping and Honing		200%	180%	100%						300%
Grinding, Diamond Turning, and Boring		200%	180%	140%	100%					300%
Broaching			200%	175%	140%	100%				200%
Reaming					175%	140%	100%			175%
Turning, Boring, Slotting, Planing, and Shaping						200%	170%	140%	100%	100%
Milling							150%	125%	100%	100%
Drilling									175%	100%

[a]Reproduced through the courtesy of the U.S. Army Management Engineering Training Activity, Rock Island Arsenal, Illinois.

*Follow same tolerance trends.

**Aproximate cost relationship of basic machining process.

as turning and a part size in the range of from 2.800 in. to 4.499 in., the following relative costs are given:

Tolerance (in.)	Relative Cost
0.008	1.0
0.005	1.4
0.003	1.7
0.002	2.0

So the extra skill and effort required to meet a tolerance of 0.002 in. results in process costs which are twice as great as for a tolerance of 0.008 in.

Similarly, for grinding a part in the same size range, we find the following relative costs:

Tolerance (in.)	Relative Cost
0.0012	1.0
0.0008	1.4
0.0006	1.8
0.0005	2.0

In this case, the cost of meeting a tolerance of 0.0005 in. will be twice as great as that for a tolerance of 0.0012 in.

In addition, the various processes have different basic costs relative to one another, and these are given in the end column as

Process	Relative Cost
Turning	1.00
Reaming	1.75
Broaching	2.00
Grinding	3.00

This would indicate grinding to be three times as costly as turning as a metal-removing process.

Table 1-2 and Figure 1–1 have been constructed from the data given by Hansen by converting the relative percentages within each process to the relative percentages between the processes. Turning was left as the base process ranging from 100% to 200% depending on the tolerance, but the 100% for reaming became 175% (the value of reaming relative to turning). so that its three values changed from 100%, 140%, and 175% to 175%, 245%, and 306%. In the same way, 100% for broaching became 200%, and 100% for grinding became 300%.

In addition, the percentage values have been changed to ratios or multipliers so that everything is compared to a value of 1.00 for turning a part of that particular size to a tolerance of 0.008 in. Table 1-2 then shows the four processes and their various tolerances on the same relative scale and permits their visual comparison when plotted in graphical form, as in Figure 1-1.

The graph shows that as we move toward closer and closer tolerances, we must move to more and more costly processes. The lines for the various processes do not all coincide or form a continuous curve, but this is simply another example of the variation which we must contend with in industry. Although there is a range of cost for any given tolerance, or a range of tolerance at any given cost, nevertheless, the rapidly increasing upward trend in cost at smaller tolerances is quite apparent.

It may be necessary to update these various process costs to bring them into line with technological changes, but the general principle will still apply and the cost of the more refined processes will be found to be multiples of the costs of the simpler processes.

This example has been taken from the metal-cutting industry, but again, the same general principles apply in other industries as well.

The axes of the graph could have been named Quality of Design instead of Tolerance, and Process Cost instead of Relative Cost. If this were done, however, the quality axis would be written in reverse; that is, instead of lowest tolerance to the left of the axis, we would have lowest quality, and instead of highest tolerance to the right of the axis, we would have highest quality. This is simply to comply with the usual convention in graph drawing, and the effect is to have the graph sloping upward to the right, instead of downward to the right. This particular method of drawing the cost curve is used in the following section.

1-8   MARGINAL QUALITY OF DESIGN

Once we are aware of the fact that increasing the quality of design also increases the manufacturing or process costs, we are likely to

Table 1-2   RELATIVE COSTS OF QUALITY FOR VARIOUS MACHINE SHOP PROCESSES[a]

Process	Relative Cost of Processes	Tolerance								
		0.0005	0.0006	0.0008	0.0012	0.002	0.003	0.005	0.008
Turning	1.00					2.00	1.70	1.40	1.00
Reaming	1.75				3.06	2.45	1.75		
Broaching	2.00		4.00	3.50	2.80	2.00			
Grinding	3.00	6.00	5.40	4.20	3.00				

[a] Part size range = 2.800 in. to 4.499 in.

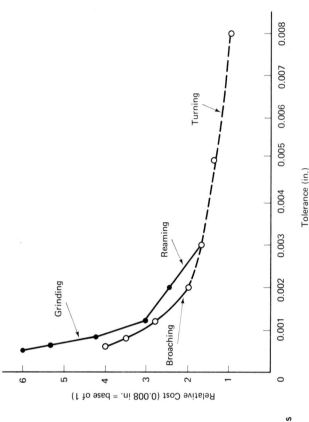

Figure 1–1   Cost-Tolerance Relationships for Machine-Shop Processes

12

think twice when someone suggests that the product be made to the highest level of quality technically possible. The question which immediately comes to mind is, "Can we sell that level of quality?"

One of the characteristics of the marketplace is that higher quality has higher market value, but this value increases at a decreasing rate. This is said to be due to increasing reluctance on the part of the buyer to pay more money for what is virtually the same product. It is represented by a rising curve, which tends to flatten off at the top. Figure 1-2(a) is a diagrammatic representation of how a typical value curve might look relative to a typical cost-of-quality curve for a particular product. It can be seen that as more money is spent on increasing the quality of design, the cost of quality increases at an increasing rate, while market value of that quality increases at a decreasing rate.

As long as the increase in value is greater than the increase in cost for a given increase in quality, then it will pay to increase the level of quality. If the increase in cost were greater than the increase in market value for a given increase in quality, then not all the added costs would be recovered in the selling price, and it would not make good business sense to make such a move.

The marginal quality is the point at which for a given increase in cost there is an equal increase in value, and this is the point at which the market dictates that we should operate.

In Figure 1-2(b), an increase in quality from point 4 to point 5 produces an increase in relative cost of from 3.0 to 3.4 (a difference of 0.4) and an increase in value of from 5.4 to 6.6 (a difference of 1.2). The increase in cost is less than the increase in value, and it is, therefore, desirable to make the indicated increase in quality.

In Figure 1-2(d) an increase in quality from level 6 to level 7 produces an increase in relative cost of from 4.0 to 4.8 (a difference of 0.8), and an increase in relative value of from 7.2 to 7.6 (a difference of 0.4). In this case, the increase in cost is greater than the increase in market vlaue and the quality change should not, therefore, be made.

In the case of Figure 1-2(c), an increase in the quality level from 5 to 6 produces an equal increase of 0.6 in both cost and value. This is the marginal quality level and is the level which should be aimed at for this particular product.

Most companies will be able to construct a cost of quality curve, but not all will have the market research resources to construct the value curve. Nevertheless, the principle still applies, and most man-

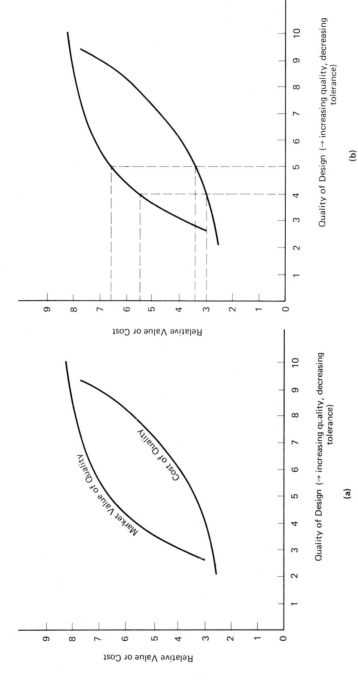

Figure 1–2 (a–d) Market Value of Quality Versus Cost of Quality of Design

14

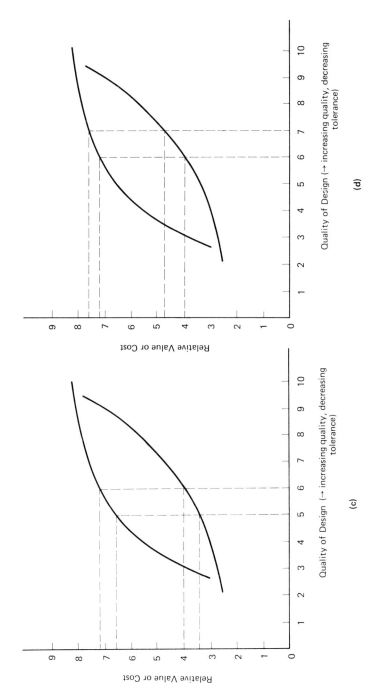

Figure 1-2 (continued)

15

agers who have a "feel" for the market in which they operate instinctively know that such an optimum quality level exists even if they may not be sure if at any given time their product is at, above, or below this value.

1-9   OPTIMUM QUALITY OF CONFORMANCE

When a manufacturing plant has the task of producing an item to a given specification, rejects will occur from time to time when the specification limits are exceeded. Each item which is rejected causes increases in the manufacturing costs through loss of productive labor hours and losses in direct and indirect materials. We have seen, however, that different manufacturing processes can operate within different specification limits, and if rejects are being produced, one solution might be to use a more refined process.

We know that the more refined process will have a higher relative cost, but we also know that each reduction in items rejected will cause a reduction in reject costs. That is, as process costs rise, the reject costs drop, and a point is reached for any given product and processes at which the sum of these two costs is at a minimum. Figure 1-3 is an example of such a relationship, and shows a minimum total cost occurring at a quality level of 1.9% rejects. The implication of this is that the company will minimize its operating costs if it will accept 1.9% rejects as an acceptable quality level, and will use a process which is appropriate for this quality level. To quote a very old saying, "You cannot make a silk purse out of a sow's ear," and you cannot, by putting pressure on people, get more out of a process than it is capable of giving. Any company producing a standard product would find it to their advantage to construct a set of curves similar to those in Figure 1-3. Companies producing a range of products, however, will not have a single cost of rejects curve, but a whole series of lines, each having a different slope. In such a case, it might be found to be sufficient to draw the two extreme cases and thus determine the range rather than the point of optimum quality of conformance. Figure 1-4 might be an example of such a case where the optimum quality of conformance is somewhere in the range of from 1.75% to 2.00% rejects.

It is important to note that this analysis is based on the assumption that the rejected items are found by the inspection department and do not leave the plant. The costs of rejects are, therefore, only internal costs and do not reflect the even more serious

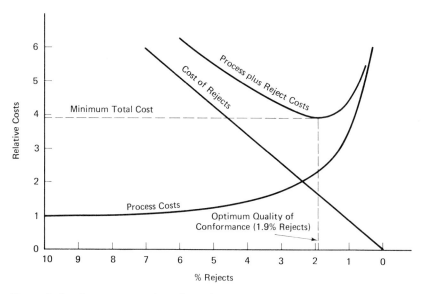

Figure 1–3 Optimum Quality of Conformance

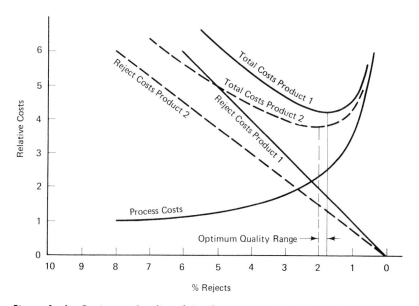

Figure 1–4 Optimum Quality of Conformance: Multiple Products

condition when rejects are not detected until after they reach the customer. The costs here are more nebulous and do not lend themselves to precise graphing, but they must nevertheless be considered. They include the loss of goodwill, or even the complete loss of a customer, and in extreme cases may result in legal action and claims for liability.

These are potential costs only, and they represent the reasons for having a sound quality-control system. Only real, in-plant, identifiable costs are used, however, in the optimization analysis.

1-10   THE QUALITY-CONTROL DEPARTMENT

When personnel from a variety of companies get together to discuss the subject of quality control, it is not uncommon to run into pointless arguments in which people talk at cross purposes about the responsibilities of the quality-control department. The reason for this is simply that the term "quality control" means different things in different industries. This difference can be particularly evident if we are comparing an assembly plant and a process plant.

The function of quality control is often broken down into a number of aspects for organizational purposes, and some or all of these may fall in the same department.

1. First there is the initial setting of process variables by which the form of the raw materials or parts will be changed into a new product or material.
2. Then there is the sampling and testing, or inspection, of the product. This may take place only at the final stage, or it may occur at a number of intermediate stages before or during production.
3. Another aspect is the collection, tabulation, and analysis of the data which has been collected.
4. The fourth aspect of the quality-control function is the making of adjustments to the process, when necessary, to bring the results into line with a predetermined specification.

In a manufacturing plant, aspects 1 and 4 may be the responsibility of the production or manufacturing department; aspect 2 may fall under the inspection department; and only the third aspect, the collection, tabulation and analysis of data, may be described as quality control.

In a process plant on the other hand, all four functions may be the responsibility of one department, which may be called the process engineering department, the technology department, the process control department, or the quality-control department, to mention only a few possibilities. It is the need in some process industries for rapid corrective action at intermediate stages in the process that necessitates the organization of all four aspects under one department. This gives shorter lines of communication and less chance of an out-of-control condition going unnoticed.

There are, of course, many other variations, and it is also not uncommon to find inspection, tabulation, and analysis of data (i.e., aspects 2 and 3) brought together in a quality-control department and all technological aspects in another department.

It is certainly not difficult to see why personnel in different industries may sometimes talk at cross purposes when they talk about quality control, but for our purposes in this book, we will confine ourselves to one aspect only. The technology involved varies from industry to industry, but the collection, tabulation, charting, and analysis of data have certain features which are common to all industries. It is the universality of this collection and analysis of data which allows it to be treated as a separate subject, and it is this subject which is dealt with in the balance of this text.

QUESTIONS AND PROBLEMS

---

1. Fully describe the following terms, giving examples of each: (a) an attribute; (b) a variable.

2. What is the general procedure described in this chapter by means of which we will attempt to measure and control the quality of a variable?

3. (a) What is meant by the term "a quality characteristic?"
   (b) List as many as possible of the quality characteristics which may be generated in the manufacture of the following items:
   (1) A cast-iron engine block.
   (2) A bolt of drapery fabric.
   (3) A can of fruit.
   (4) A 40-cm-diameter aluminum frypan.
   (5) A shut-off valve for a water line.
   (c) Name one attribute for each of the above products which might result in rework or rejection of the item.

4. Name the four sources of variation in a quality characteristic and state how each contributes to the final amount of variation found in the end product.

5. (a) Item 1 has a nominal size of 1.250 in. and a tolerance of ± 0.001 in. Item 2 has a nominal size of 1.250 in. and a tolerance of ± 0.004 in. Which item has the higher quality of design?
   (b) Give an example of a difference in quality of conformance from two production centers producing the same item.
   (c) Describe the interrelationship which can exist between quality of performance, quality of design, and quality of conformance.

6. (a) Draw a graph indicating the general condition for marginal quality of design. (A relative scale of units must be used to illustrate the concept correctly.)
   (b) What is marginal quality of design?

7. (a) Draw a graph which illustrates optimum quality of conformance. (Proper graph-drawing technique is essential to the correct identification of this value.)
   (b) What is optimum quality of conformance?

2

The Measurement of Variation

2-1 *IN THE LONG RUN*

A coin has one head and one tail, so when we toss one we expect that 50% of the time it will land head up, and 50% of the time it will land tail up. Or do we really expect this? Is there not something missing in the first statement?

The statement is definitely incomplete, for we know full well that if we flipped a coin ten times and got exactly five heads and five tails, we would be extremely surprised. We would be even more surprised if we flipped the coin in the air 10,000 times and it landed head up exactly 5,000 times and tail up exactly 5,000 times.

The trouble with the first statement is that we have ignored the fact that the events are controlled by chance. By this we mean that each event (a head or a tail) has an equal **opportunity** of occurring. This does not mean that each will occur an equal number of times. What it means is that, **in the long run,** the number of events will **tend** to be equal. So if we toss the coin a large enough number of times, we can expect the number of heads to **approach** 50% of the total number of tosses.

This concept of a long-run tendency is fundamental to most of the statistical concepts which are to follow. Over and over again, statements are made about the amount of variation to be expected in a given variable, and these statements are often only correct **in the long run.** So if we are to avoid one of the first pitfalls in the interpretation of statistical quality-control data, we must keep the words **in the long run** constantly in mind.

2-2   ABSOLUTE AND RELATIVE ERROR

If, on tossing a coin 100 times, we obtained 55 heads and 45 tails, we might describe the deviation from the long-run expected value in a number of ways. We might say that the excess of heads over tails was 10, or we might say that the *error* was plus or minus 5. In this type of usage, there is no suggestion of a "mistake" as such in the word "error," but simply a deviation from an aimed-at or expected value.

Now suppose that we tossed the coin 10,000 times and obtained 5,020 heads and 4,980 tails. In this case, we have an error of ±20. Does this mean that the error is greater than when we only flipped the coin 100 times? The answer depends on whether we are interested in the absolute number of the deviation or in the deviation relative to the aimed-at value.

There are, therefore, two common ways of describing deviations from an expected value. One is the *absolute error*, which is the actual number by which we deviate from the aimed-at value, and the other is the *relative error*, which is the absolute error expressed as a percentage of the aimed-at value. In the case of the two coin-tossing cases already described, the value would be as follows:

Number of Trials	Number of Heads		Absolute Error	Relative Error
	Actual	Expected		
100	55	50	5	10 %
10,000	5,020	5,000	20	0.4%

So, in the second case, although the absolute error is four times as great as in the first, the relative error is only four hundredths ($\frac{4}{100}$) of the first.

When we relate these concepts to manufacturing, we find that it is usually when small numbers are being produced, or when human life is dependent upon the product, that we are interested in absolute error. In most statistical applications in industry, we are concerned with large numbers or with production over a long period of time, and in these circumstances the relative error is appropriate. In fact, later in this chapter we will introduce a special case of relative error which is of particular value when comparing a number of different quality characteristics.

2-3   MEAN DEVIATION

Although the terms absolute and relative error are likely to be found in common usage in industrial measurement, the terms *absolute* and *relative deviation* are equally as appropriate. In fact, in many cases, the terms are interchangeable.

If we have a number of items, all made to the same nominal size, we might tabulate them as in Table 2-1.

Table 2-1   SHAFT SIZE: DEVIATION FROM NOMINAL

Nominal Shaft Size (in.)	Actual Shaft Size	Deviation (from Nominal)
1.000	1.004	+ 0.004
1.000	1.001	+ 0.001
1.000	0.997	− 0.003
1.000	1.005	+ 0.005
1.000	0.991	− 0.009
1.000	1.001	+ 0.001
1.000	1.004	+ 0.004
1.000	1.002	+ 0.002
1.000	1.003	+ 0.003
1.000	1.002	+ 0.002

This tabulation draws attention to the fact that an error or deviation not only has a numerical or absolute value, but also has a sign. It is positive if it is greater than the aimed-at value, and it is negative if it is less than the aimed-at value.

In Table 2-1 there are only two negative values, indicating that the majority of the values are greater than the nominal size, but we might reasonably expect that, if the variation were uniform about the mean, the positive and negative values would cancel each other out. The positive values here, however, have a sum of +0.022, and the negative values a sum of −0.012 for a balance of +0.01.

If we want to find the mean (or arithmetical average) of the actual shaft diameters, we add up all the values and divide by the number of shafts. Doing this, we obtain a total of 10.01 and a mean diameter of 1.001 in. This tells us the mean of an assortment of numbers, but it says nothing about the amount of deviation, so we might do the same thing with the deviations, add them up (ignoring sign), and divide by 10. The sum of the absolute deviations comes to 0.034, for a mean deviation of 0.0034.

Since the mean shaft diameter is 0.001 in. greater than nominal size, it would be of interest to find out how much the values deviate from the mean rather than from the nominal size. The new values for deviation are shown in Table 2-2. In this case, the sum of the absolute deviations comes to 0.028, giving a mean deviation of only 0.0028 in., and, as we expected, the positive values are canceled out by the negative values.

$$\text{Sum of positive deviations} = +0.014 \text{ in.}$$
$$\text{Sum of negative deviations} = -0.014 \text{ in.}$$

Taking the sum of the absolute values of deviation and dividing by the number of cases gives a value for the mean deviation. This then is another way of reporting the amount of variation in a group of values, but it has limited practical application. As with relative error, it is a value which stands by itself and is of limited use in making subsequent mathematical deductions.

Table 2-2   SHAFT SIZE: DEVIATION FROM MEAN

Mean Shaft Diameter (in.)	Actual Shaft Diameter	Deviation (from Mean)
1.001	1.004	+0.003
1.001	1.001	Nil
1.001	0.997	−0.004
1.001	1.005	+0.004
1.001	0.991	−0.010
1.001	1.001	Nil
1.001	1.004	+0.003
1.001	1.002	+0.001
1.001	1.003	+0.002
1.001	1.002	+0.001

2-4   STANDARD DEVIATION

The most commonly known expression of average is the *arithmetical mean*, which we have already used to find the mean diameter of a number of shafts and the mean deviation of the various shaft sizes from a standard value. In statistics, however, we use a variety of methods for describing a position of central tendency in a collection of numbers.

The *mode*, for example, is the most commonly occurring value, while the value which has as many observations below it as there are above it is called the *median*. It is only when the deviations are uniformly distributed about the center that the mean, median, and mode coincide. Another form of average is the *harmonic mean*, which is used when averaging rates of any kind (e.g., miles/hour, cents/ pound, pounds/square inch, etc.), and this is the reciprocal of the arithmetic mean of the reciprocals of all the values.

Still another is the square root of the mean of the squares, and this is the basis of the *standard deviation*. To be more precise, the standard deviation is a mean value for deviation which is described as the *root-mean-squared deviation*. In symbols it is written as follows:

$$\sigma = \sqrt{\frac{\Sigma(x - \mu)^2}{n - 1}}$$

where σ (sigma) = standard deviation
μ (mu) = mean of all values
x = individual values
n = number of values involved
Σ (capital sigma) = sum of all values following the sign

$(x - \mu)$ is the deviation of the individual values from the mean, and this is the same as that used to find mean deviation in the previous section. In this case, however, the square of each deviation is calculated and then the sum is found for all the squares. The mean of the squares is found by dividing by the numbr of values (less 1), and the square root of this mean then gives the standard deviation.*

It is a good rule never to use complex methods when simple ones are equally as effective, so there must be a very good reason for using the root-mean-squared deviation rather than the mean deviation. The reason is that when the mean and the standard deviation are known for a set of values we can apply probability theory and can calculate the probability of observations falling above or below any specific value. It is the ability to do this which enables

---

* Subtracting 1 from the number of values is a statistical correction which is necessary to prevent understatement of the deviation in small samples. Obviously, as n becomes larger, the effect of subtracting 1 becomes insignificant.

us to make precise statements about the capabilities of industrial processes and about deviations which occur during the operation of industrial processes.

2-5   BASIC CALCULATION OF STANDARD DEVIATION

A thorough understanding of the description or definition of standard deviation should enable anyone to set up a table for its computation. The following are the steps which would be taken when the number of observations is not too large. The shaft diameters used for the calculation of mean deviation are used as an example.

STEP 1

List the individual values in a column (x values).

Shaft Diameter (in.)

x
1.004
1.001
0.997
1.005
0.991
1.001
1.004
1.002
1.003
1.002

STEP 2

Find the sum of the individual values.

x
1.004
1.001
0.997
1.005
0.991
1.001
1.004
1.002
1.003
1.002
$\Sigma x = 10.010$

STEP 3

Divide the sum by the number of values to find the mean.

$$\bar{x} = \frac{\Sigma x}{n} = \frac{10.010}{10} = 1.001 \text{ in.}$$

Note: (1) When all the values in a given population of observations are known, the symbol μ (mu) is used for the mean, but when we are only dealing with a sample or part of a population, the symbol $\bar{x}$ (read "x bar") is used. (2) In quality-control work we seldom know the true value for μ because we seldom have a complete population to study. Values are produced in intermittent batches or on a continuous basis, and we do not have the whole population until the order runs out. We therefore put together all the sample data as it is generated and, **in the long run,** the cumulative value for $\bar{x}$ will tend to approach the true value for the population.

STEP 4

Find the deviation of each value from the mean.

x	$x - \bar{x}$
1.004	+0.003
1.001	0
0.997	−0.004
1.005	+0.004
0.991	−0.010
1.001	0
1.004	+0.003
1.002	+0.001
1.003	+0.002
1.002	+0.001

Note: Up to this point the steps are the same as for the calculation of mean deviation.

STEP 5

Calculate the squares of the deviations and find their sums.

x	$(x - \bar{x})$	$(x - \bar{x})^2$
1.004	$+0.003$	0.000009
1.001	0	0
0.997	-0.004	0.000016
1.005	$+0.004$	0.000016
0.991	-0.010	0.000100
1.001	0	0
1.004	$+0.003$	0.000009
1.002	$+0.001$	0.000001
1.003	$+0.002$	0.000004
1.002	$+0.001$	0.000001
	$\Sigma (x - \bar{x})^2 =$	0.000156

The step-by-step build-up of the table has been used here for illustrative purposes only; normally the table would be set up immediately as in step 5.

STEP 6

Find the mean of the squared deviations by dividing $\Sigma (x - \bar{x})^2$ by $(n - 1)$.

$$\frac{\Sigma (x - x)^2}{(n - 1)} = \frac{0.000156}{9} = 0.0000173$$

STEP 7

Calculate standard deviation by finding the square root of the value found at step 6.

$$\text{Standard deviation} = \sqrt{\frac{\Sigma (x - \bar{x})^2}{n - 1}} = \sqrt{0.0000173}$$

$$= 0.0042 \text{ in.}$$

Note: (1) When all the values in a given population are known, the symbol σ (sigma) is used to denote standard deviation, but when only a part of the population is being considered, the letter s is used. (2) As was the case with the mean, we seldom know the true value for σ in quality-control work and therefore use the value for s from the cumulative samples.

The preceding method is derived directly from the formula, or definition, and is straightforward and simple to use when the number of observations is not too large and when the numerical values of the observations are neither extremely large nor extremely small.

If 200 or 300 observations were involved, the tabulated values could conceivably cover over 20 pages, and the time involved in the computations could be excessive. If the differences in values were numerically in the tens of thousands, then the squares of the differences would be in the hundreds of millions, making the calculations awkward and perhaps exceeding the capacity of some of the simpler pocket calculators. For these reasons, shortcut methods have been developed which not only reduce the time consumed in performing the calculations, but also tend to reduce the risk of error during the calculations.

2-6   SHORTCUT METHODS FOR CALCULATING STANDARD DEVIATION

2-6.1   Coded Procedure

Suppose that it is necessary to calculate the mean and standard deviation for the set of values shown in Table 2-3 for the percentage of silicon content of a cast iron. The basic method would be too lengthy and would entail 50 lines in the tabulation.

Table 2-3   PERCENT OF SILICON CONTENT IN A CAST IRON

2.03	2.04	2.05	2.06	2.07	2.08
2.09	2.10	2.11	2.12	2.13	2.04
2.05	2.06	2.07	2.08	2.09	2.10
2.11	2.05	2.06	2.07	2.08	2.09
2.10	2.11	2.06	2.07	2.08	2.09
2.10	2.11	2.06	2.07	2.08	2.09
2.10	2.06	2.07	2.08	2.09	2.10
2.07	2.08	2.09	2.10	2.07	2.08
2.08	2.07				

STEP 1

One method of approach would be to start by listing all of the available values from smallest to largest.

STEP 2

Check off the frequency of occurrence of each value and list under f.

x	f
2.03	1
2.04	2
2.05	3
2.06	6
2.07	9
2.08	9
2.09	7
2.10	7
2.11	4
2.12	1
2.13	1

STEP 3

Select a value near the median and call this the *assumed mean*. Designate it by the symbol x_0. In this case, let $x_0 = 2.08\%$.

STEP 4

Assign the value zero to x_0 and plus or minus values to all other x values depending on whether they are greater or less than x_0. List these under d.

x	f	d
2.03	1	-5
2.04	2	-4
2.05	3	-3
2.06	6	-2
2.07	9	-1
2.08	9	0
2.09	7	$+1$
2.10	7	$+2$
2.11	4	$+3$
2.12	1	$+4$
2.13	1	$+5$

STEP 5

Tabulate fd and fd^2.

> Note: fd^2 is not the same as $(fd)^2$. When tabulating fd multiply f by d. When tabulating fd^2, multiply fd again by d.

The complete table is as follows:

x	f	d	fd	fd²
2.03	1	-5	-5	25
2.04	2	-4	-8	32
2.05	3	-3	-9	27
2.06	6	-2	-12	24
2.07	9	-1	-9	9
2.08	9	0	0	0
2.09	7	$+1$	$+7$	7
2.10	7	$+2$	$+14$	28
2.11	4	$+3$	$+12$	36
2.12	1	$+4$	$+4$	16
2.13	1	$+5$	$+5$	25
	$\Sigma f = 50$		$\Sigma fd = 1$	$\Sigma fd^2 = 229$

STEP 6

Find Σf, Σfd, and Σfd^2.

STEP 7

Using the following formulas, calculate $\bar{x}$ and s.

$$\bar{x} = x_0 + C \cdot \frac{\Sigma fd}{\Sigma f},$$
where C is the numerical interval between each value or group of values

$$= 2.08 + 0.01 \frac{(-1)}{50}$$

$$= 2.08 - 0.0002$$

$$= 2.08\%$$

(Note: 0.0002 is insignificant as it rounds off to zero at both the second and third decimal places.)

$$s = C \cdot \sqrt{\frac{\Sigma f d^2}{\Sigma f} - \left(\frac{\Sigma f d}{\Sigma f}\right)^2}$$

$$= 0.01 \sqrt{\frac{229}{50} - \left(\frac{-1}{50}\right)^2}$$

$$= 0.01 \sqrt{4.58 - 0.0004}$$

$$= 0.01 \sqrt{4.58}$$

$$= 0.021\%$$

2-6.2   Grouped Frequency: Coded Procedure

When the observed values vary to a greater extent than in the preceding example, they may be arranged in small subgroups or classes and treated as having the values of the mid-points (or mid-marks) of each class. Any error introduced by making this assumption is so slight as to have no practical significance.

This procedure would be applicable for a collection of data such as the information in Table 2-4 on the ultimate tensile strength (pounds/square inch) of a class 50 cast iron. The steps to be used in arranging this data in a systematic manner are as follows:

Table 2-4   ULTIMATE TENSILE STRENGTH OF CLASS 50 CAST IRON (lb/in.^{2})

55,300	55,300	52,900	54,000	52,300
52,100	52,700	56,700	50,300	50,100
54,800	53,300	56,500	53,300	51,300
51,700	53,100	51,500	52,700	51,200
50,500	51,300	51,900	52,000	52,600
52,500	52,900	55,800	55,600	55,000
56,100	54,000	51,000	52,100	53,000
53,500	53,700	53,100	53,200	54,200
54,300	50,700	51,400	52,200	52,900
53,500	53,100	53,400	55,000	54,500
55,600	55,800	51,500	56,000	54,000
54,200	54,100	53,300	53,600	55,500
55,000	52,200	52,800	54,200	55,400
54,900	53,500	54,200	54,300	55,700
52,400	53,200	54,600	54,000	52,900
52,600	54,800	54,500	53,600	53,900
54,000	53,500	52,800	52,500	53,700
52,800	53,300	52,000	52,700	54,000

STEP 1

Find the total numerical range in the values by subtracting the minimum value from the maximum value. That is,

$$\text{Range} = 56,700 - 50,100$$

$$= 6,600$$

STEP 2

Each subgroup or class of values must encompass an equal numerical portion of this range, so we must decide on the size of this portion, or *class interval*. This class interval (i) is dependent not only upon the numerical range, but also upon the total number of values, and some people decide on its value by subjective judgment based on experience. For the inexperienced, however, a simple formula exists, which involves first of all finding the number of classes.

$$\text{Number of classes} = 1 + 3.322 \text{ (log of total frequencies)}$$

$$= 1 + 3.322 \text{ (log } \Sigma \text{ } f)$$

In our example this would give

$$\text{Number of classes} = 1 + 3.322 \text{ (log 90)}$$

$$= 1 + (3.322 \times 1.954)$$

$$= 1 + 6.49$$

$$= 7.49$$

Rounding to the nearest odd number gives a value of 7.

STEP 3

Divide the range by the number of classes less 1, to obtain the class interval. That is,

$$\text{Class interval} = \frac{6600}{7\text{-}1}$$

$$= \frac{6600}{6}$$

$$= 1100$$

STEP 4

To ensure that the lowest and highest values are centered in their classes, subtract half the class interval from the lowest value and designate this as the first class boundary. That is,

$$50,100 - 550 = 49,550$$

Add the class interval (1,100) to this to obtain the upper boundary for the first class.

$$49,550 + 1,100 = 50,650$$

This then becomes the lower boundary for the second class, and 1,100 is added to obtain the upper boundary for the second class. This procedure is continued until all the class boundaries have been tabulated. Class mid-marks are tabulated at the same time.

If any alternative method is used to determine class boundaries, it is most important to ensure that the boundaries are unambiguous. There must never be any doubt into which class an observation should fall, and to ensure this it is good practice to express the boundaries to one more significant figure than the measurements.

STEP 5

Check off each observed value against its appropriate class.

Class Boundaries	Class Mid-Marks	Check Marks	f
49,550 to 50,650	50,100	III	3
50,650 to 51,750	51,200	JHT IIII	9
51,750 to 52,850	52,300	JHT JHT JHT IIII	19
52,850 to 53,950	53,400	JHT JHT JHT JHT IIII	24
53,950 to 55,050	54,500	JHT JHT JHT JHT II	22
55,050 to 56,150	55,600	JHT JHT I	11
56,150 to 57,250	56,700	II	2
			$\Sigma f = 90$

Beyond this point the steps are the same as those for the Coded Procedure. In this example, the assumed mean is taken at the median value of 53,400 lb/in.^{2} and we obtain the following:

Class Mid-Marks	f	d	fd	fd^2
50,100	3	-3	-9	27
51,200	9	-2	-18	36
52,300	19	-1	-19	19
53,400	24	0	0	0
54,500	22	$+1$	$+22$	22
55,600	11	$+2$	$+22$	44
56,700	2	$+3$	$+6$	18
	$\Sigma f = 90$		$\Sigma fd = +4$	$\Sigma fd^2 = 166$

STEP 6

$$\bar{x} = x_0 + C \cdot \frac{\Sigma fd}{\Sigma f}$$

$$= 53,400 + 1100 \times \frac{4}{90}$$

$$= 53,449 \text{ lb/ in.}^2$$

$$s = C \cdot \sqrt{\frac{\Sigma fd^2}{\Sigma f} - \left(\frac{\Sigma fd}{\Sigma f}\right)^2}$$

$$= 1,100 \sqrt{\frac{166}{90} - \left(\frac{4}{90}\right)^2}$$

$$= 1,100 \sqrt{1.84 - 0.002}$$

$$= 1,491 \text{ lb/ in.}^2$$

This method is extremely flexible and permits wide differences in the number of classes used. For example, if by subjective judgment we had decided to use 11 instead of 7 classes, the results would have been as follows:

STEP 3(a)

$$\text{Class interval} = \frac{6600}{11 - 1}$$

$$= 660$$

STEP 5(a)

Class Boundaries	Class Mid-Marks	Check Marks	f
49,770 to 50,430	50,100	II	2
50,430 to 51,090	50,760	III	3
51,090 to 51,750	51,420	JHT II	7
51,750 to 52,410	52,080	JHT IIII	9
52,410 to 53,070	52,740	JHT JHT JHT	15
53,070 to 53,730	53,400	JHT JHT JHT III	18
53,730 to 54,390	54,060	JHT JHT IIII	14
54,390 to 55,050	54,720	JHT IIII	9
55,050 to 55,710	55,380	JHT II	7
55,710 to 56,370	56,040	IIII	4
56,370 to 57,030	56,700	II	2

With the assumed mean at the median value of 53,400, the final table is as follows:

STEP 6(a)

Class Mid-Marks	f	d	fd	fd²
50,100	2	−5	−10	50
50,760	3	−4	−12	48
51,420	7	−3	−21	63
52,080	9	−2	−18	36
52,740	15	−1	−15	15
53,400	18	0	0	0
54,060	14	+1	+14	14
54,720	9	+2	+18	36
55,380	7	+3	+21	63
56,040	4	+4	+16	64
56,700	2	+5	+10	50
	$\Sigma f = 90$		$\Sigma fd = +3$	$\Sigma fd^2 = 439$

STEP 7(a)

$$\bar{x} = x_0 + C \cdot \frac{\Sigma fd}{\Sigma f}$$

$$= 53,400 + \left(660 \times \frac{3}{90} \right)$$

$$= 53,400 + 22$$

$$= 53,422 \text{ lb./in.}^2$$

$$s = C \cdot \sqrt{\frac{\Sigma fd^2}{\Sigma f} - \left(\frac{\Sigma fd}{\Sigma f}\right)^2}$$

$$= 660 \sqrt{\frac{439}{90} - \left(\frac{3}{90}\right)^2}$$

$$= 660 \sqrt{4.878 - 0.001}$$

$$= 660 \sqrt{4.877}$$

$$= 1,458 \text{ lb/in.}^2$$

Comparing these two sets of results we have:

	$\bar{x}$	s
Using 7 classes	53,449	1,491
Using 11 classes	53,422	1,458
Absolute error	27	33
Relative error	0.05%	2.2%

These relative differences are not great enough to be of any practical significance, showing that there is wide latitude in the choice of the number of classes. The strength values have been measured to the nearest 100, but the differences between values are only in the 10s, so if we round to the nearest measurable accuracy the two pairs of results become the same: 53,449 and 53,422 both round off to 53,400 lb/in.² and 1,491 and 1,458 both round off to 1,500 lb/in.². The relative error of 2.2% is therefore of no practical significance.

When followed in a systematic manner, this method is a great time saver. If an attempt had been made to use the basic method, the square of the difference between the mean and the lowest number would be found to be 11,035,684, and the ensuing computations would obviously have been laborious. (*Note:* 53,422 − 50,100 = 3,322; 3,322² = 11,035,684.)

2-6.3   The Electronic Calculator

Electronic pocket calculators have had such an impact on the lives of those doing computational work that it would be inappropriate to discuss shortcut methods without reference to these instruments. The very simple models which add, subtract, multiply, and divide are of little assistance in quality-control work, but those which provide square and square root functions help considerably in the types of calculations shown in the previous sections. With parentheses it is possible to calculate.

$$c \cdot \sqrt{\frac{\Sigma\,fd^2}{\Sigma f} - \left(\frac{\Sigma\,fd}{\Sigma f}\right)^2}$$

in one continuous operation without the need for the intermediate steps shown in the examples. Here, again, time can be saved when a large number of calculations are being performed.

Perhaps the greatest shortcut of all is to be found with those calculators which provide statistical functions directly without the need for the operator to use any formulas or tabulations other than the original list of values. There are numerous moderately priced models on the market which perform these functions.

With a number of these instruments it is only necessary to depress the Xn key after each x value has been entered and, after all the data are in, press $\bar{x}$ to obtain the mean and s to obtain the standard deviation. The three examples given in this chapter were processed in this manner with the following results:

	x	s
Shaft diameter	1.0009	0.0039
Percent of silicon content	2.080	0.022
Tensile strength	53,441	1,473

The number of digits displayed in calculators has produced a problem among some users which has become known as "delusions of accuracy," where every single digit in the display is reported. This is not acceptable practice. We cannot, by performing a calculation, produce results which are more accurate than the original measurements. So if the original measurements were to the third decimal place, good mathematical practice dictates that the mean and standard deviation should also be to the third decimal place. If the original measurements were to the nearest 100 lb/in.^{2}, the results should also be to the nearest 100 lb/in.^{2}.

One exception to this rule, however, is made in quality-control work. It is frequently useful to be unambiguous about whether an observation falls above or below the mean value and, to accomplish this, it is necessary to report the mean with one more significant figure than is found in the original x values. That is, if measurements were to the third decimal place, it is permissible to report the mean to the fourth decimal place; if measurements were to the nearest thousand, it is permissible to report the mean to the nearest hundred.

Using this practice, the calculator results compare with the formula results as follows:

| | Mean | | Absolute Difference | Relative Difference |
	Formula	Calculator		
Shaft diameter	1.0010	1.0009	0.0001	0.01%
Percent silicon	2.080	2.080	Nil	Nil
Tensile strength	53,450	53,440	10	0.02%

| | Standard Deviation | | Absolute Difference | Relative Difference |
	Formula	Calculator		
Shaft diameter	0.004	0.004	Nil	Nil
Percent silicon	0.02	0.02	Nil	Nil
Tensile strength	1,490	1,470	20	1.3%

There is again no difference of any practicable significance between the results obtained directly from the calculator and those obtained either by the basic or shortcut methods.

It might seem that the expanded use of calculators would make the other shortcut methods of only academic interest, but we must be aware of the fact that there is one important piece of information which the calculator does not provide. If we look at the check marks at steps 5 and 5(a) of the grouped frequency coded procedure, we obtain a visual impression of the distribution of values. The calculator does not provide this visual impression. It does not tell us if there are two modes, or if there are gaps in the distribution, or if the mean is closer to one end of the range than the other (skewed), and there are times when this information is useful to have.

2-7   COEFFICIENT OF VARIATION

When a number of quality characteristics are generated by one process, it is sometimes useful to know which has the greatest relative
amount of variation. Characteristics with larger numerical values
will tend to have numerically larger standard deviations, but, as we
have already seen, a large absolute amount does not necessarily
mean a large relative amount, and to make comparisons on a uniform basis, the standard deviation is expressed as a percentage of
the mean for each characteristic. This relationship is known as the
coefficient of variation and is given the symbol v.

$$v = \frac{s}{\bar{x}} \times 100$$

For example,

$$\text{Shaft diameter: } v = \frac{0.004}{1.001} \times 100 = 0.4\%$$

$$\text{Percent silicon: } v = \frac{0.02}{2.08} \times 100 = 1.0\%$$

$$\text{Tensile strength: } v = \frac{1,470}{53,440} \times 100 = 2.8\%$$

Knowing which characteristics have the highest coefficients of variation may be useful information for a quality-improvement program
or when decisions are being made about product or process specialization.

QUESTIONS AND PROBLEMS

---

1. In a batch of 5,000 items, 25 were rejected because of defects.
   What is
   (a) The absolute level of rejects;
   (b) the relative level of rejects?

2. Find the mean absolute deviation for the following set of values
   for an item having a nominal size of 5.00 cm: 5.040, 5.010, 4.972,
   5.051, 4.955, 5.011, 5.042, 5.024, 5.036, 5.028.
   (a) Find the mean absolute deviation from the mean.
   (b) Find the mean absolute deviation from the nominal size.

3. Using the values in question 2, calculate the standard deviation using the basic method.

4. The following 50 values are the percentage of total carbon content in class 50 cast iron:

3.19	3.09	3.04	3.17	3.24
3.16	3.25	3.32	3.08	3.09
3.37	3.25	3.11	3.39	3.14
3.10	3.21	3.14	3.18	2.96
3.14	3.25	3.09	3.18	3.29
3.21	3.14	3.13	3.42	3.33
3.29	3.24	3.17	3.18	3.14
3.34	3.26	3.30	3.28	3.25
3.28	3.35	3.36	3.12	3.11
3.11	3.27	3.21	3.37	3.27

(a) Using the grouped frequency coded procedure calculate the mean and standard deviation of this set of results.

(b) Calculate the coefficient of variation.

5. Describe an advantage and a disadvantage in the use of an electronic calculator for the direct calculation of mean and standard deviation for a set of values.

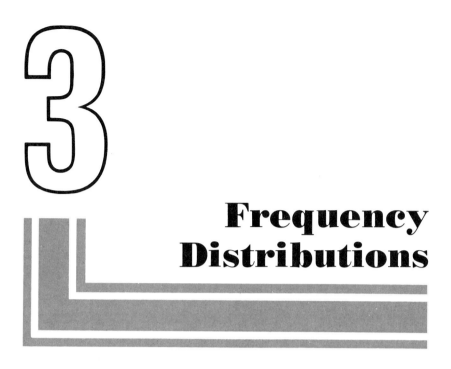

Frequency Distributions

3-1 THE HISTOGRAM: ABSOLUTE FREQUENCY

One disadvantage of using an electronic calculator for directly determining mean and standard deviation is the fact that it does not give a visual impression of the distribution of values. This visual impression, or pictorial presentation, is often useful to have and is generally in the form of either a histogram or a frequency-distribution curve.

If we take the tally marks, or check marks, from step 5 or step 5(a) in the calculations for tensile strength in Section 2-6-2 and turn them counterclockwise through 90 degrees, we would have the x values on the horizontal axis and the frequency values on the vertical axis, as shown in Figures 3-1 and 3-2, respectively. This is the conventional way of presenting this type of data, except that, instead of check marks, the frequency values are shown as straight lines or vertical rectangles whose lengths are proportional to their numerical values and whose widths are proportional to their class intervals. Figures 3-3 and 3-4 are arranged in this way and are known as histograms. A casual look at these two histograms might lead to the

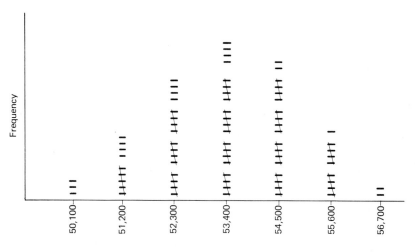

Tensile Strength Class Mid-Marks

Figure 3–1   Tensile Strength Frequency Check Marks from Step 5

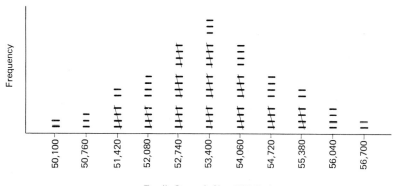

Tensile Strength Class Mid-Marks

Figure 3–2   Tensile Strength Frequency Check Marks from Step 5A

conclusion that they represent two different sets of data, but in fact they represent the same data arranged in different ways. The two diagrams are visual presentations of data which are not directly comparable.

   If we wanted to compare the distributions of data from two years ago with data from a year ago and data from the present time, we could do this by means of histograms provided that they were all drawn to the same scale and all had an equal size of class interval. The means and standard deviations would most likely be different and, hence, the class boundaries would not be the same, but the histograms could legitimately be compared with one another. Changes in either the class interval or the scale of the diagrams would void any visual comparisons.

Considering the care that is necessary when comparing data on the same quality characteristic, it is obvious that even more care would be required if we were to try to compare different quality characteristics. In fact, unless we follow certain strict rules, it should not be done. There is a way out of this dilemma, however, and that is to have the horizontal axis represent not the actual values of the

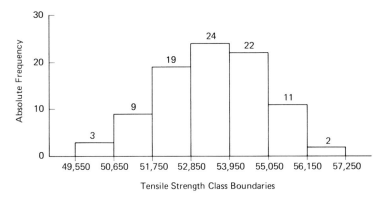

Figure 3-3   Tensile Strength Histogram for Seven Classes

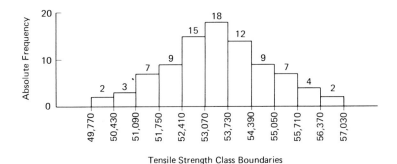

Figure 3-4   Tensile Strength Histogram for Eleven Classes

variable, but its standard deviation. If the class intervals were all some fixed fraction of the standard deviation for each characteristic, then histograms would provide useful visual comparisons.

3-2   THE HISTOGRAM: RELATIVE FREQUENCY

Before any comparisons at all can be made, there is one other problem which must be resolved. We are very often interested in comparing the distributions for different sizes of samples or populations, and when we do this the absolute values of the frequencies could be very misleading. They would tend to show higher values for the larger samples and lower values for the smaller ones.

To overcome this difficulty, the frequencies are generally expressed in relative terms as either a percentage or a decimal of the total number of values. The relative frequencies of occurrence of the various classes in the tensile strength data are shown in Tables 3-1 and 3-2, and the 11 classes are shown pictorially in Figure 3-5. Obviously, in this case, there is little change in the numerical value for the frequency as the sample size (90) was so close to 100. However, in most cases, the change is more dramatic.

Table 3-1   RELATIVE FREQUENCY OF TENSILE STRENGTH DATA USING SEVEN CLASSES

Class Mid-Mark	Absolute Frequency	Relative Frequency	
		Percent	Fraction
50,100	3	3.33	0.0333
51,200	9	10.00	0.1000
52,300	19	21.11	0.2111
53,400	24	26.67	0.2667
54,500	22	24.44	0.2444
55,600	11	12.22	0.1222
56,700	2	2.22	0.0222
Total	90	99.99	0.9999

If we take a much smaller sample, however, such as that in Table 2-3 for the silicon content in a cast iron, we find that the difference becomes more noticeable. Table 3-3 shows the absolute

Table 3-2 RELATIVE FREQUENCY OF TENSILE STRENGTH DATA
USING ELEVEN CLASSES

Class Mid-Mark	Absolute Frequency	Relative Frequency	
		Percent	Fraction
50,100	2	2	0.02
50,760	3	3	0.03
51,420	7	8	0.08
52,080	9	10	0.10
52,740	15	17	0.17
53,400	18	20	0.20
54,060	14	16	0.16
54,720	9	10	0.10
55,380	7	8	0.08
56,040	4	4	0.04
56,700	2	2	0.02
Total	90	100	1.00

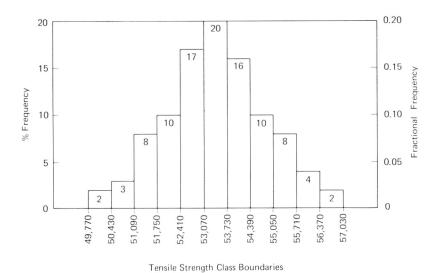

Tensile Strength Class Boundaries

Figure 3-5 Tensile Strength Histogram: Relative Frequency

Table 3-3 RELATIVE FREQUENCY OF SILICON CONTENT IN A
CAST IRON

Class Mid-Mark	Absolute Frequency	Relative Frequency Percent	Fraction
2.03	1	2	0.02
2.04	2	4	0.04
2.05	3	6	0.06
2.06	6	12	0.12
2.07	9	18	0.18
2.08	9	18	0.18
2.09	7	14	0.14
2.10	7	14	0.14
2.11	4	8	0.08
2.12	1	2	0.02
2.13	1	2	0.02
Total	50	100	1.00

and relative frequencies for this set of data, and Figures 3-6 and
3-7 show a noticeable difference between the histograms for the absolute and relative frequencies, respectively.

3-3   COMPARING HISTOGRAMS

Figures 3-4 and 3-6 are both histograms of absolute frequencies of
two characteristics arranged in 11 classes and cannot be compared

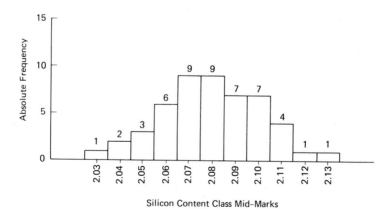

Silicon Content Class Mid-Marks

Figure 3–6 Silicon Content Histogram: Absolute Frequency

with one another because of the large difference in the sample sizes. Figures 3-5 and 3-7, on the other hand, are of relative frequencies, and an attempt might be made to make a limited comparison of the two.

The differences are quite apparent, but the similarities may not be. Some of these differences may be due to the limited size of the sample of silicon values and the fact that each class represents only a single analytical value, whereas the tensile classes each represent a range in values. This again might have been resolved had the class intervals in each case been based on their respective standard deviations.

One of the obvious similarities is that the frequency of occurrence of values rises from a low, for x values less than the mean, to a maximum at or near the mean, and then drops again to a low for values greater than the mean. This, we will find, is a good general description of most of the distributions which we will be studying.

Not quite so obvious is the similarity in the concentration of frequencies which we find in the middle and at the ends of each of the two examples. If we sum the frequencies for the three middle classes (i.e., the median and the class on either side), we find 53% of the tensile values and 50% of the silicon values in this position. If we sum the two end classes at the low end and the two at the high

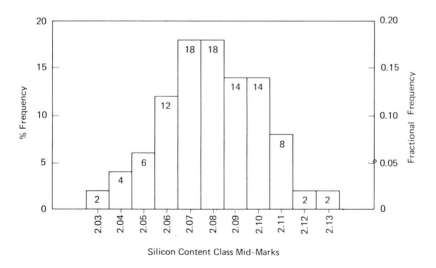

Figure 3–7 Silicon Content Histogram: Relative Frequency

end of the range, we find 11% of the tensile values and 10% of the silicon values.

It might have been thought that we were comparing "apples" and "oranges," and that we could not possibly find any similarities between two such dissimilar characteristics as a physical property and a chemical content, but here in the distribution of their values we find the suggestion of a very interesting similarity. At this point the similarities in the concentrations of values can only be taken as a qualitative similarity, but it is a clue to a very important property of distributions which we will examine in a quantitative manner in Chapter 4.

3-4   THE FREQUENCY CURVE

One disadvantage of the histogram is that it gives the visual impression of discrete steps from one x value to another, but we know that this is not correct. We are engaged in the study of variables, and a variable can have any possible value in a continuum of values. If some relationship exists between the x values and the frequency of their occurrence, then it would be much more correct to show this as a continuous line or curve passing through (or close to) the known points.

In Figures 3-8 and 3-9 the frequencies have been plotted against the class mid-marks for the tensile strength example and a smooth line drawn through the points. In both cases, the left side of each curve is almost a mirror image of the right side, and there are only two points on each which do not exactly coincide with the smoothly drawn line.

When silicon content frequencies are plotted in Figure 3-10, a smooth curve, with one side being the mirror image of the other, can still be drawn, but in this case, there is more of a scatter to the points. There are as many above the line as there are below it.

This method of presenting the data now gives a visual impression of gradual changes in the frequency of occurrence of values rather than abrupt changes.

3-5   THE NORMAL DISTRIBUTION

The scatter in Figure 3-10 is due to the fact that the curve represents a theoretical condition which is possible "in the long run," whereas

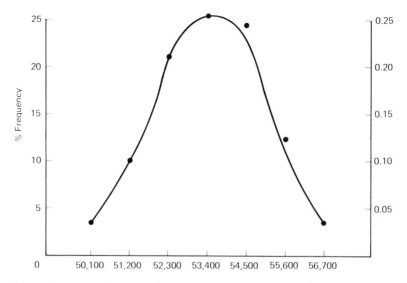

Figure 3-8   Tensile Strength Frequency Curve: Seven Classes

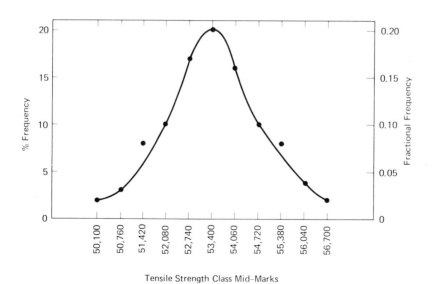

Tensile Strength Class Mid-Marks

Figure 3-9   Tensile Strength Frequency Curve: Eleven Classes

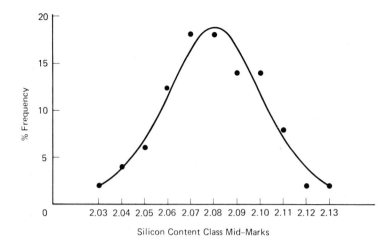

Figure 3–10   Silicon Content Frequency Curve

the points represent the values for our limited sample. **Samples have this disadvantage: they are only approximate representations of the entire population of all possible values and are not the population itself.** If we were to continue to take more samples, we would find that the mean, standard deviation, and frequency distributions would vary slightly from one another, but that eventually they would stabilize at steady values and give a curve similar to the one shown.

The final curve would be of the form known as the *normal curve,* and distributions of values which conform to the normal curve are known as *normal distributions.* Naturally occurring and manufacturing variables frequently conform to this type of distribution. Where the quality characteristic is a variable with no constraints on either the low or the high end of the scale, then it is most likely to be represented, **in the long run,** by the normal distribution. That is, the normal distribution applies when most of the values cluster around the mean and there is an equal, though remote, chance of finding extremely small and extremely large values.

It was stated earlier that the reason for using standard deviation rather than some other measure of dispersion was that it permitted the application of probability theory. It is through the characteristics of the normal curve that this can be done, but first we must look at the nature of the curve itself.

The fact is that there is not just one normal curve; there are an infinite number of normal curves. There is a normal curve for each standard deviation and its accompanying mean. The curves in Figures 3-8 through 3-10 were simply drawn by hand, but accurate curves for each set of conditions can be plotted from the following formula:

$$f(x) = \frac{e^{-\left(\frac{(x-\mu)^2}{2\sigma^2}\right)}}{\sigma\sqrt{2\pi}}$$

(Note that $\left[-\left(\dfrac{(x-\mu)^2}{2\sigma^2}\right)\right]$ is the power to which e is raised.)

where $f(x)$ = frequency for any given value of x
  x = value whose frequency is being determined
  μ = mean
  σ = standard deviation
  π = constant 3.14159
  e = constant 2.71828

π and e are constants, so the parameters of the formula are μ and σ, and any change in either of these results in a different frequency for x and, hence, a different curve.

  To draw a curve for a particular case, selected values of x are chosen to cover a range of about ±3.5 standard deviations from the mean, and the respective values of frequency are obtained. The x and f values are then plotted and the curve drawn. Obviously, these calculations would be somewhat complex and rather time consuming, but the matter has been simplified by the use of standard tables (see Appendix 1) and by the use of preprogrammed calculators.

3-6   THE STANDARDIZED NORMAL VARIABLE

It would be impracticable to prepare tables for an infinite range of means combined with an infinite range of standard deviations. This difficulty is overcome, however, by finding the difference between each x value and its mean and relating this difference to the size of the standard deviation. The difference between any x value and the mean will be some fraction or multiple of the standard deviation, and it is this standardized version of the difference for which tables have been prepared. It is known as the *standardized normal variable* (or sometimes as the standardized normal *deviate*) and is designated by the letter z.

$$z = \frac{x - \mu}{\sigma}, \qquad \text{for the population}$$

or $\qquad\qquad z = \frac{x - \bar{x}}{s}, \qquad \text{for a sample}$

The procedure then is to subtract the mean from the x value, divide by the standard deviation to find the z value, and then look up the frequency from the tables. Sufficient x values are selected to cover the required range and facilitate the drawing of a smooth curve.

When x is less than the mean, the value of z will be negative, but as the curve is uniform on both sides of the mean, there is no need to tabulate both positive and negative z values. The absolute value of z gives the frequency for that value whether it be less than or greater than the mean. For example;

$$\bar{x} = 50,000$$

$$s = 1,500$$

when $\qquad\qquad x = 45,000,$

$$z = \frac{45,000 - 50,000}{1,500}$$

$$= -\frac{5,000}{1,500}$$

$$= -3.33$$

when $\qquad\qquad x = 55,000,$

$$z = \frac{55,000 - 50,000}{1,500}$$

$$= \frac{5,000}{1,500}$$

$$= 3.33$$

The frequency in both cases is found from the tables to be 0.00156.

Using this procedure we can now construct a table of values for the tensile strength example which we have already studied.

$$\text{Tensile strength mean} = 53{,}422 \text{ lb/in.}^2$$

$$\text{Tensile strength standard deviation} = 1{,}458 \text{ lb/in.}^2$$

These values produce the curve shown in Figure 3-11. It is drawn to the same scale as Figure 3-8 and is fairly similar in shape to both Figures 3-8 and 3-9. In Figure 3-8 with seven classes, the maximum frequency at the mean is 0.2667; in Figure 3-9 with 11 classes, it is 0.20, while in the normal curve it has a value of 0.399.

What is the reason for this apparent conflict and confusion among the various diagrams? It is, once again, that, first, our figures are for a sample which is **approximately normal,** and, second, the arbitrary choice of the size of the class interval places varying ranges of values at each plotted point. The normal curve is plotted from information for **individual** values.

If we are careful to observe the warning given in Section 3-1 and maintain equal class intervals, then we can use frequency curves to compare the distributions of values from samples taken from dif-

Table 3-4   z VALUES FOR TENSILE STRENGTH

Class Mid-Marks (x)	x − x̄	z	f
48,120	− 5,302	− 3.64	0.00053
48,780	− 4,642	− 3.19	0.00246
49,440	− 3,982	− 2.73	0.00961
50,100	− 3,322	− 2.28	0.02965
50,760	− 2,662	− 1.83	0.07477
51,420	− 2,002	− 1.37	0.15608
52,080	− 1,342	− 0.92	0.26129
52,740	− 682	− 0.47	0.35723
53,400	− 22	− 0.02	0.39886
54,060	638	0.44	0.36213
54,720	1,298	0.89	0.26848
55,380	1,958	1.34	0.16256
56,040	2,619	1.80	0.07895
56,700	3,278	2.25	0.03174
57,360	3,938	2.70	0.01042
58,020	4,598	3.16	0.00271
58,680	5,258	3.61	0.00059

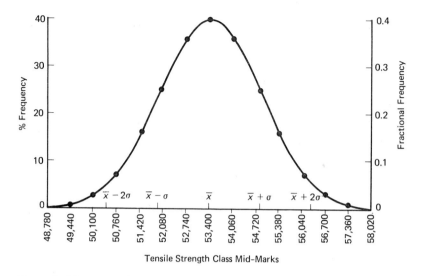

Figure 3–11 Normal Curve Based on Tensile Strength Data

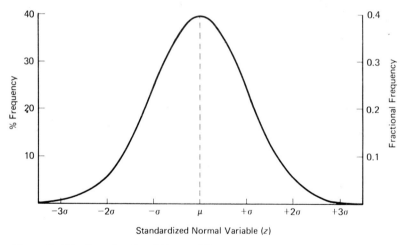

Standardized Normal Variable (z)

Figure 3–12 Standardized Normal Curve

ferent lots or at different periods of time. On the other hand, if we are confident that the population is normally distributed, then the normal curve can provide us with more information, in the long run.

Finally, if we draw the normal curve with z values along the horizontal axis instead of the values for one particular variable, then we have a curve which has universal application for all variables. Figure 3-12 has been drawn directly from the information contained in the tables with no reference to any particular variable whatsoever. Notice that, although the curve appears to reach zero at its extreme ends, the table shows clearly that the values become very small, but only tend toward zero and do not actually reach it. It will be seen later, however, that for most practical purposes the frequency can be assumed to be zero beyond a certain point.

QUESTIONS AND PROBLEMS

---

1. If we wish to compare data for a quality characteristic from different periods of time or from different production centers, and we desire to do this by means of histograms, what factors must be held constant if the histograms are to be truly comparable?

2. Show the following results pictorially in the following ways:
   (a) As a histogram of absolute frequencies.
   (b) As a histogram of relative frequencies.
   (c) As a relative frequency curve with the variable on the x axis.
   (d) As a relative frequency curve with standard deviation values on the x axis.

Percent of Carbon in Class 50 Cast Iron

3.19	3.09	3.04	3.17	3.24	3.01
3.16	3.25	3.32	3.08	3.09	3.16
3.37	3.25	3.11	3.39	3.14	3.03
3.10	3.21	3.14	3.18	2.96	3.18
3.14	3.25	3.09	3.18	3.29	3.20
3.21	3.14	3.13	3.42	3.33	3.05
3.29	3.24	3.17	3.18	3.14	3.22
3.34	3.26	3.30	3.28	3.25	3.07
3.28	3.35	3.36	3.12	3.11	3.17
3.11	3.27	3.21	3.37	3.27	3.21

3. Assume that the values in question 2 are taken from a normal distribution and draw the appropriate normal curve. Superimpose this curve on the curve drawn in question 2(d).

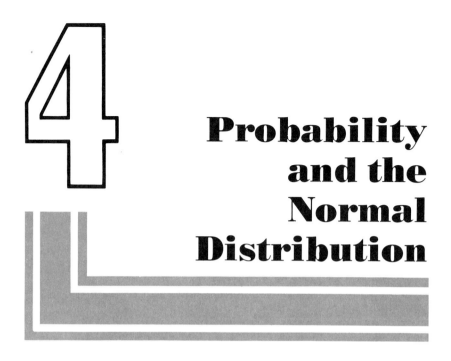

Probability
and the
Normal
Distribution

4-1 TOSSING A COIN

A coin has one head and one tail, and when it is given a spin and allowed to fall freely onto a surface, it will land with either the head or the tail uppermost. The outcome of the trial (or experiment) can have no other value and we say that the two events (heads and tails) are mutually exclusive. That is, when one occurs the other cannot occur.

As we observed in Section 2-1 we can expect that **in the long run** 50% of the outcomes will be heads and 50% will be tails. Probabilities, however, are generally expressed as decimals, so we would say that there is a 0.5 probability of getting a head and a 0.5 probability of getting a tail.

The use of decimals for probabilities means that we have a range of from 0 to 1 for any event. Zero means that the event is impossible and 1 indicates certainty. All values between 0 and 1 indicate that fraction of certainty that we ascribe to the event.

Another way of expressing probabilities is to say that as a head is one of two equal possibilities that there is one chance in two of getting a head. There would, of course, also be one chance in two of getting a tail.

We have, therefore, three ways of describing the probability òf the outcome of an event. We can say that there is a chance of **1 in 2** of it occurring; we can say that there is a **0.5 probability** of it occurring; and we can say that it will occur **50% of the time, in the long run.** Each of these expressions has its own particular application.

4-2   SAMPLE SPACE

We say that the sample space consists of the set of all possible outcomes of an experiment and in the case of the coin toss this would be two, a head and a tail. These events are mutually exclusive, and one of the laws of probability says that the sum of the probabilities of mutually exclusive events is unity, or certainty. That is:

Probability of obtaining a head **or** a tail

$$= \text{probability of a head} + \text{probability of a tail}$$

$$= 0.5 + 0.5$$

$$= 1$$

In other words, we are **certain** to get **either** a head or a tail.

If we throw a single die, there is one chance in six of getting any particular number uppermost and

$$\text{Probability of getting any number} = \frac{1}{6} + \frac{1}{6} + \frac{1}{6}$$

$$+ \frac{1}{6} + \frac{1}{6} + \frac{1}{6}$$

$$= 1$$

If we cut off each edge of a cube so that the surfaces were equal, we would have an 18-sided object and a probability of 1 in 18 that any one side would be uppermost, and if we could make a 1,000-sided object, we would have 1 chance in 1,000 that one side would be uppermost.

These outcomes, however, are all in nice round whole numbers, but we are studying variables which can have fractional numbers and extremely small probabilities of being at some particular fractional number. We would, therefore, have to try to imagine the equivalent of an object with an extremely large number of sides and, therefore, an extremely small probability of any one particular side occurring.

The more sides we cut from our equal-sided object, the closer and closer it will approach the shape of a sphere. In fact, the sphere is the limiting case for this type of probability, where there is an equal opportunity for any one point of surface being uppermost, but where that probability is infinitely small.

If we restrict the movement of the sphere to only one plane, we have the same condition as rolling a ring. If we imagine the ring to be in a slot so that it will not fall over, then there is an equal, though small, probability of any one point being uppermost when it stops rolling. Drawing a circle on a page would be a graphical way of representing this type of probability condition.

Unfortunately, any given value in a continuum of values for a variable may **not** have an equal probability of occurring. In fact there is usually a greater probability of finding values close to the mean than of finding values which are very much smaller or very much larger than the mean, and the probabilities for a variable are represented graphically, not by a circle, but by the **normal curve.**

4-3   THE NORMAL CURVE

The height of the normal curve represents the relative frequency of occurrence of the various values, the width represents the amount of deviation of an x value from the mean, and, **the area under the curve, between the mean and the x value, represents the probability of finding values in that range.**

There is little point to inquiring into the probability of some exact value. We are dealing with a continuum of value, and even close to the mean any one value will have a rather small probability of occurring. What we are really interested in, in quality-control work, is knowing the probability of being above or below some specific value. For example, if there is a maximum value to the permissible content of some impurity in our product, what is the probability of **exceeding** that maximum specification? Or if there is a minimum strength which our product must have, what is the probability of being **below** this specification? The normal distribution can provide answers to these questions.

Certainty is represented by a probability of 1, and, as the total area under the curve represents the total of all possible occurrences, this area is given the value of 1. It is, in other words, a certainty that the values will occur somewhere between negative infinity and positive infinity.

The curve is uniform about the mean, so anything we say about the negative side will hold true for the positive side, and vice versa. Also, as the mean is in the center of the distribution, 50% of the area is on the negative and 50% on the positive side of the mean. That is, there is a 0.5 probability of being between the mean and the negative infinity and a 0.5 probability of being between the mean and positive infinity.

If the normal curve were a horizontal straight line, then anything we said about the area under one segment would be the same for any other equal length of segment. Unfortunately, the normal curve slopes downward, and its slope changes throughout its length. Because of this, the area between the mean and one standard deviation is not the same as the area between one and two standard deviations, and this also is not the same as the area between two and three standard deviations. In fact, the values are

Area between mean and one standard deviation = 0.341

Area between one and two standard deviations = 0.136

Area between two and three standard deviations = 0.021

To simplify the use of the normal distribution for probability problems, areas have been calculated for small increments of z values. These are to be found in the center column of Appendix 1. To use the table, we must first know the values for mean and standard deviation, and knowing the x value we are interested in, we then calculate z. We then look for the z value in Appendix 1, and beside it we find the value for the area between the mean and our specific x value. As the area and the probability are directly proportional, the value for area now becomes our value for probability. For example;

$$\text{Mean} = 50{,}000 \text{ psi}$$

$$\text{Standard deviation} = 1{,}500 \text{ psi}$$

$$x = 47{,}000 \text{ psi}$$

$$z = \frac{x - \bar{x}}{s}$$

$$= \frac{47{,}000 - 50{,}000}{1{,}500}$$

$$= -\frac{3{,}000}{1{,}500}$$

$$= -2.00$$

Looking in the tables we find that at $z = 2.00$ the area between the mean and our chosen x value is 0.47725. That is, there is a 0.47725 probability that values will fall between 50,000 and 47,000 psi. Or we could say that, in the long run, 47.725% of the results will fall between 47,000 and 50,000 psi.

4-4   ONE-TAILED RISKS

We mentioned earlier that we frequently want to know the probability of being above some maximum specification limit or below some minimum specification limit. Each of these represents *one-tailed* risks, as we can only be off specification in one direction. Where only a maximum value is specified, there is no risk of being off specification by being extremely low, and where only a minimum is specified there is no risk of being off specification by being extremely high.

In the preceding example, if 47,000 psi had been the minimum specification, then we would have less interest in the probability of being between the mean and the minimum than we would have in being less than the minimum, and the tables do not give this. However, it is very easy to find.

The area from the mean to negative infinity is 0.5, and the area from the mean to the minimum specification value is 0.47725, so the area beyond the minimum is the difference between the two. Thus

Area below the minimum specification $= 0.5 - 0.47725$

$$= 0.02275$$

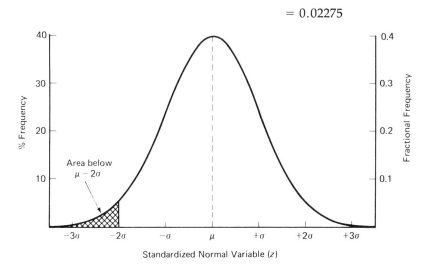

Figure 4–1   Standardized Normal Curve: Negative One-Tailed Risk

In other words, we could expect that **in the long run** 2.3% of the results would fall below the minimum specification. The cross-hatched area in Figure 4-1 is the area of probability in this case and represents the 2.3% of the cases which will tend to be below specification.

Similarly, if we had a maximum specification of 0.030% sulfur in our product with a mean running at 0.028% and a standard deviation of 0.001%, what is the probability of finding results which are off specification?

$$\text{Mean} = 0.0285\%$$

$$\text{Standard deviation} = 0.001\%$$

$$x = 0.030\%$$

$$z = \frac{x - \bar{x}}{s}$$

$$= \frac{0.030 - 0.0285}{0.001}$$

$$= \frac{0.0015}{0.001}$$

$$= 1.50$$

Looking in the tables we find that the area between $\bar{x}$ and x at a z value of 1.5 is 0.43319 and the area beyond $x = 0.5 - 0.43319$, or 0.06681. That is, **in the long run** we could expect that 6.7% of the product would be off specification owing to an unacceptably high sulfur value. The cross-hatched area in Figure 4-2 is the area of probability in this case and represents the 6.7% of the cases which will tend to be above specification.

4-5   TWO-TAILED RISKS

Not every quality characteristic has a specification which limits the amount of variation in only one direction. Many have specifications which impose a minimum and a maximum to the range of variation. In these cases, we speak of having a *two-tailed* risk, as there is a probability of being below specification and a probability of being above specification.

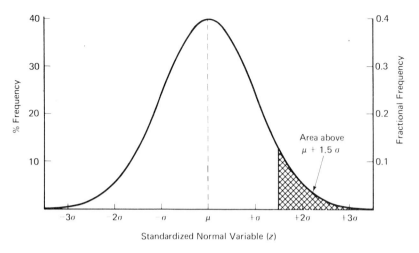

% Frequency

Fractional Frequency

Area above
$\mu + 1.5\,\sigma$

-3σ -2σ $-\sigma$ μ $+\sigma$ $+2\sigma$ $+3\sigma$

Standardized Normal Variable (z)

Figure 4–2 Standardized Normal Curve: Positive One-Tailed Risk

Machined items frequently involve two-tailed risks, and a dimension stated as 0.500 ± 0.005 in. would be such a case. The dimension is aimed at 0.500 in., but it is acceptable within the range of from 0.495 to 0.505 in. Suppose in this case the process mean is the same as the aimed-at value of 0.500 in., and the standard deviation is 0.002 in.; what is the probability of being off specification?

$$\text{Mean} = 0.500 \text{ in.}$$

$$\text{Standard deviation} = 0.002 \text{ in.}$$

$$x = 0.505 \text{ in.}$$

$$z = \frac{x - \bar{x}}{s}$$

$$= \frac{0.505 - 0.500}{0.002}$$

$$= \frac{0.005}{0.002}$$

$$= 2.5$$

Looking in the tables we find that the area between $\bar{x}$ and x at a z value of 2.5 is 0.49379 and, therefore, the area beyond $x = 0.5 -$ 0.49379, or 0.00621. That is, the probability of being above specifi-

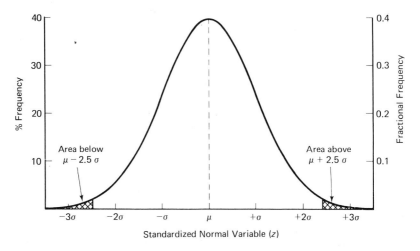

Figure 4-3 Standardized Normal Curve: Two-Tailed Risk

cation is 0.00621. But this is a two-tailed risk so there is an equal opportunity of being below specification, and the sum of the two gives the total probability of being either above or below specification. Thus

Probability of being off specification $= 0.00621 + 0.00621$

$$= 0.01242$$

In other words, **in the long run** we can expect that 1.2% of the product will fail to meet specifications. The two cross-hatched areas in Figure 4-3 are the areas of probability in this case and represent the 0.6% of the cases which will tend to be below specification and the 0.6% which will tend to be above specification.

In summary, the procedure is as follows:

4-5.1 To Find the Probability of a Value Being in the Interval from Mean to x

1. Determine μ or $\bar{x}$.

2. Determine the standard deviation.

3. Calculate z for the value of x in question.

4. In the tables of areas under the normal curve, find the area for the value of z found in step 3. This fraction of the area under

the curve is the probability of the occurrence of an event in the stated interval.

5. If the problem involves $\pm x$, the value from the table must be multiplied by 2.

4-5.2 To Find the Probability of Results Being Beyond a Value of x

1. Determine mean, standard deviation, and z as in Section 4-5.1.

2. Find the area under the curve between the mean and x.

3. Subtract the probability of an occurrence between the mean and x from 0.5 to obtain the probability of an event with a value beyond that of x (i.e., less than or greater than x, as the case may be).

4. If the problem involves $\pm x$, the value found at step 3 must be multiplied by 2.

4-6 CONFIDENCE LEVELS

When we have a known value of x, such as a specification limit, we find z and then the probabilities involved, but in some areas of quality control we work in the opposite direction. In these cases, we start by deciding on an acceptable probability level and then find the variable values which will be the limits for this level of probability. This acceptable probability level is known as the *confidence level* and describes the percentage of all results that we would expect to find within specified limits, **in the long run.** These limits can be found by looking in the table in Appendix 1 in the reverse order. That is, if we have a two-tailed risk and we want to be confident that 99% of the time the outcomes will fall within the specified limits we must first remember that the table covers only half of the area under the curve and we are, therefore, looking for half of 99% or 49.5%. This is expressed as a decimal in the tables and will, therefore, be 0.495. We then look down column 2 until we find the value closest to 0.495, and this is seen to be 0.49506. Looking across to the z column, we find that this corresponds to a z value of 2.58. In other words, if we want to set limits which will include 99% of all results, these should be set at ± 2.58 standard deviations.

For example, if we take the example from Section 4-3 where the mean is 50,000 psi and the standard deviation is 1,500 psi and decide that we want to set limits at the 99% confidence level, we must multiply 1,500 by 2.58. This puts the limits at 50,000 ± 3,870 psi, or

Minimum value = 46,130 psi

Maximum value = 53,870 psi

In the long run, 99% of the strength measurements will fall between these limits.

Confidence levels are not chosen in a haphazard manner. There are certain commonly accepted values used in quality control and other areas of applied statistics. Table 4-1 has been prepared in order to compare some confidence levels which are frequently referred to and to note the influence of the type of risk which is involved (i.e., one- or two-tailed risk). Note that the probabilities are shown two ways, as long-run percentages and as ratios (or odds).

One of the traps which a student will often fall into is attempting to read a table such as Table 4-1 as though it were the written word. The eye traverses the rows and the columns and perceives only a mass of numbers. The student then gives up on any attempt to interpret the numbers and moves on to the next paragraph of the text material. This is most unfortunate, as much useful information can be contained in tables of this type, and the student should develop the habit of taking a systematic approach to data of this type.

If we first look at the Percentage Falling within the Limits, we see that in each case, for any one multiple of the standard deviation, there is a greater percentage included in a one-tailed than in a two-tailed risk. The reason for this is that there are no limitations on one side of the distribution with a one-tailed risk. For example, if we look in the tables for the area contained between the mean and 1.96 standard deviations we find that to be 0.475. With a two-tailed risk we set limits at plus 1.96 and at minus 1.96, so we double the 0.475 and get 0.950 or 95.0%. With a one-tailed risk we have a limit at **either** plus **or** minus 1.96, so on the side of the mean with no constraints we have half the area under the curve, and only on the constrained side do we have 0.475. The total area for a one-tailed risk in this case is, therefore, 0.5 + 0.475 (i.e., 0.975 or 97.5%). This difference occurs through all the values for standard deviation, but it becomes progressively less as we go up the scale.

At one standard deviation the difference is 15.865%.

At two standard deviations the difference is 2.275%.

At three standard deviations the difference is 0.135%.

At 3.87 standard deviations the difference is 0.005%.

Table 4-1 NORMAL PROBABILITIES AND STANDARD DEVIATION LIMITS

Multiples of Standard Deviation Risk		1	1.65	1.96	2	2.33	2.58	3	3.09	3.29	3.71	3.87
Percentage falling within the limits	One-tailed	84.135	95.00	97.50	97.725	99.0	99.5	99.865	99.9	99.95	99.99	99.995
	Two-tailed	68.27	90.00	95.00	95.45	98.0	99.0	99.73	99.8	99.9	99.98	99.99
Percentage falling beyond the limits	One-tailed	15.865	5.00	2.50	2.275	1.0	0.5	0.135	0.1	0.05	0.01	0.005
	Two-tailed	31.73	10.00	5.00	4.55	2.0	1.0	0.27	0.2	0.1	0.02	0.01
Ratio of results Beyond limits to total results	One-tailed	1 in 6.3	1 in 20	1 in 40	1 in 43.96	1 in 100	1 in 200	1 in 740	1 in 1000	1 in 2000	1 in 10000	1 in 20000
	Two-tailed	1 in 3.15	1 in 10	1 in 20	1 in 21.98	1 in 50	1 in 100	1 in 370	1 in 500	1 in 1000	1 in 5000	1 in 10000

Figure 4-4 shows how the confidence levels start off quite far apart at low levels of standard deviation and gradually merge toward one another until **at about three standard deviations the differences between the values become so slight that the two lines blend into one.** This flattening out of the curves above about three standard deviations also means that small differences in limits produce large differences in the probabilities of points being beyond the limits. Figure 4-5 shows this graphically, and in this case we see that the two lines tend to merge into one **below** about 2.5 standard deviations. When looking at Figure 4-5, we must remember that as we move up the vertical axis the probabilities become less and less as the numerical values become greater. **Figures 4-4 and 4-5 are simply opposite ways of looking at the same information.**

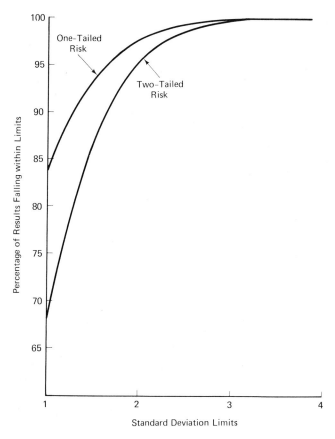

Figure 4–4 Confidence Levels For Two-Tailed and One-Tailed Risks

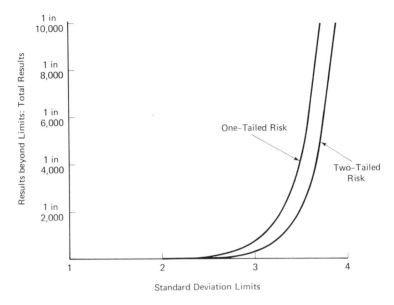

Figure 4–5 Odds in Favor of a Result Being beyond the Limits

Another feature which we can see is that whole-number standard deviation limits always give confidence levels with fractional values, and that if we want to use whole-number confidence levels we must use fractional standard deviation limits. The quality-control practice in North America is to use whole-number standard deviation limits, and $\pm 3\sigma$ is a value which we will shortly discuss in more detail. There is a tendency, however, among some people to refer to this as the 99% level, and this type of sloppy terminology must be studiously avoided. There is a considerable difference between 99.0% and 99.73% in statistical terms. It may not appear to be much of a difference in the sense of what is **included,** but when we look at what is **excluded** we see that there is indeed a considerable difference. At the 99.0% level the odds in favor of a result being either below or above specification in a two-tailed risk are **1 in 100,** while at the 99.73% level they are only **1 in 370.** It is, therefore, extremely important that we be precise in our statements about limits and levels of confidence.

4-7 PROCESS CAPABILITY

We have seen that variation is inherent in all manufacturing processes, and we have examined means whereby this variation can be measured. We have noted that industrial variation tends to conform to the normal distribution, and we have observed the characteristics of probability in this distribution. In this section, we will now put these various factors together.

When a manufacturer is asked if it would be possible to meet a certain specification, the answer may be a guess or it may be a sound probability statement. The trouble with guesses is that they are generally based on what has been happening **recently,** and this may be quite different from what will happen **in the long run.** Variations observed over a short period of time are frequently much narrower than variations over a long period of time, but new contracts to new specifications have a tendency to become long-term commitments.

A probability statement on the other hand will be based on information about the population of values and will include an implicit or explicit statement about the probability of failing to meet the specification. To do this, we compare the specification to the expected long-term range in values. This expected range in values is taken as the range from the mean minus three standard deviations to the mean plus three standard deviations and is known as the *process capability*.

$$\text{Process capability} = (\mu - 3\sigma) \text{ to } (\mu + 3\sigma)$$

If we take the example from Section 4-3, where mean = 50,000 psi and standard deviation = 1,500 psi, then

$$\text{Process capability} = 50,000 - (3 \times 1,500) \text{ to } 50,000 + (3 \times 1,500)$$

$$= (50,000 - 4,500) \text{ to } (50,000 + 4,500)$$

$$= 45,500 \text{ psi to } 54,500 \text{ psi} \quad \text{or} \quad 50,000 \pm 4,500 \text{ psi}$$

In some processes the standard deviation may remain fairly constant for a moderate range in aimed-at or mean values. Under these circumstances it may be convenient to express process capability simply as the total 6σ range. That is, the preceding case could also be correctly stated as

$$\text{Process capability} = 6 \times 1,500$$

$$= 9,000 \text{ psi}$$

Of the two methods, the first is to be preferred as it provides values which are directly comparable with a technical specification.

Plus and minus three standard deviations may appear to be an arbitrary level at which to define process capability, but in Section 4-6 we saw that it was at or about 3σ that the probability curve started to flatten out. The chance of getting a result beyond $\pm 3\sigma$ is only 1 in 370, and the odds become even more remote the farther out we go. So although there can be no hard and fast point arrived at by an examination of the normal curve, most industrial manufacturers are prepared to accept a confidence level within which the values will fall 99.73% of the time. It is impossible to set limits which will include 100% of all values, so 99.73% is a practical compromise which most industries can live with.

4-8   PROCESS CAPABILITY AND THE TECHNICAL SPECIFICATION

The question which we must now answer is, what is the most desirable relationship between process capability and the technical specification? First, let us consider the dimensional example in Section 4-5 and a specification which is narrower than the process capability.

$$\text{Mean} = 0.500 \text{ in.}$$

$$\text{Standard deviation} = 0.002 \text{ in.}$$

$$\text{Process capability} = 0.500 \pm 0.006 \text{ in.}$$

$$= 0.494 \text{ in. to } 0.506 \text{ in.}$$

If the specification calls for 0.500 in. $\pm$ 0.003 in., the dimensions will range from 0.497 in. to 0.503 in. This means that by chance alone some dimensions will fall between 0.497 in. and 0.494 in., and some dimensions will fall between 0.503 in. and 0.506 in.; we must, therefore, find the probability of this occurring.

To do this we substitute one of the specification limits for x in the z formula:

$$z = \frac{x - \bar{x}}{s}$$

$$= \frac{0.503 - 0.500}{0.002}$$

$$= \frac{0.003}{0.002}$$

$$= 1.5$$

From the tables, the probability of a value being **within** this space is 0.4332, and the probability of being **beyond** 0.503 in. is, therefore, 0.5 − 0.4332, or 0.0668 or 6.68%. This is a two-tailed risk, however, so there is an equal probability of a result being below 0.497 in. That is, **in the long run** we can expect that 13.36% of the product will be rejected because of being either above or below specification limits. Figure 4-6 illustrates this example, and the cross-hatched portions represent the areas of probability of being either above or below specification. All specifications which are narrower than the process capability will, therefore, introduce a measurable probability of some of the product failing to meet specification.

The action taken as a result of this knowledge will depend on the size of the risk and on the economics of the situation. If the probability is "low" and the selling price includes a good markup, then we may decide to ignore the risk and accept the order. If the probability is "high" and the markup is low, then we may decide to reject the order and look elsewhere for business. However, there is still another alternative. Where the market will permit it, the costs associated with the higher risk can be considered as additional manufacturing costs and the selling price then marked up from this re-

Figure 4–6   Specification Narrower Than Process Capability

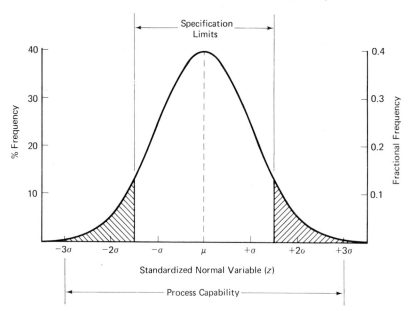

vised cost. The costs involved will include increased inspection to find and identify the off-specification material or items and the cost of either reworking or remaking the rejected product.

It is particularly important to point out here that everything that has been said about narrow specifications applies only **in the long run.** There must be a large enough order that it will be made over an extended period of time. With a small order being made over a short period of time we may have no rejected product at all, but, on the other hand, it may be double our calculated value. The short run is not necessarily representative of the long run.

Now let us look at the situation where the specification is wider than the process capability. Using the same example, but a specification which calls for 0.500 ± 0.007 in., the permissible variation will be from 0.493 in. to 0.507 in., and

$$z = \frac{0.507 - 0.500}{0.002}$$

$$= \frac{0.007}{0.002}$$

$$= 3.5$$

The probability of a value being within this space is 0.4998 or 0.9996 for both sides of the mean. The process capability will contain 99.73% of the results, and the specification will contain 99.96%, so there is an even lower chance of finding results beyond the specification limits than beyond the process capability limits. In fact, there is only 1 chance in 2,500 that a point will fall beyond the specification limits. This is a very desirable situation from the point of view of quality of conformance, and Figure 4-7 illustrates it graphically.

There is a catch to this, however. If we refer back to Section 1-9, we will see that the more refined processes tend to have the higher operating costs. So, if the process capability is **very much** narrower than the specification, there is a possibility that we are using a more refined process than is necessary and perhaps even pricing ourselves out of the business.

In summary, we can say that **a desirable specification to work to would be one which equals or slightly exceeds the range of the process capability.**

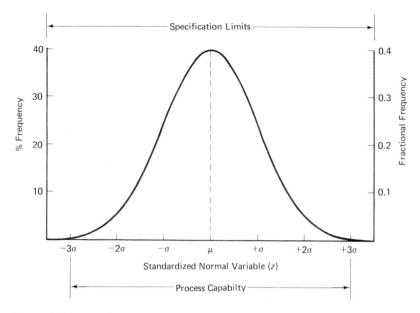

Figure 4–7   Specification Wider Than Process Capability

QUESTIONS AND PROBLEMS

---

1. An industrial process generates an average of 5% reject product. State the probability of obtaining rejects in three different ways.

2. What is the probability of the value of a variable falling in the range of from the mean to positive infinity?

3. Metal produced in a plant has a mean hardness of 200 BHN (Brinell hardness number) and a standard deviation of 6.
   (a) What is the probability of a value being between 200 and 220?
   (b) What is the probability of a value being found beyond 220 BHN? State this probability in three different ways.
   (c) If the metal is being manufactured to a specification which calls for a minimum hardness of 190 BHN, what is the probability of some of the product being off specification?

4. A cast-to-size bar has a diameter specification of 0.40 in. ± 0.015 in. The mean diameter of bars produced is 0.400 in. and the standard deviation is 0.008 in. What is the probability of producing bars which fail to meet specification?

5. A cast-to-size bar has a diameter specification of 0.40 in. ± 0.015 in. The mean diameter of bars produced is 0.408 in. and the standard deviation is 0.008 in. What is the probability of producing bars which fail to meet specification?

6. Determine the 99.73% confidence level for the bars described in question 4.

7. (a) Describe in words and symbols what is meant by the term "process capability."
   (b) What is the process capability for the bars described in question 4?

8. What is the most desirable relationship to have between process capability and the technical specification?

Taking Samples

5-1 WHY TAKE SAMPLES?

If you have ever gone shopping for a basket of apples, you have probably looked at the nice shining red apples on the top of the basket and then lifted two or three to see what the ones underneath looked like. You have taken a sample. Experience has probably taught you that the top layer is not necessarily representative of what is below; in fact, it may be what is called a **biased** sample.

A biased sample is one which contains more than its fair share of a particular segment of the population. If we think in terms of the normal distribution, a biased sample might be one consisting mainly of items with values below the mean or one consisting mainly of items with values above the mean. Neither would give a very good representation of the population as a whole, so we want to avoid taking biased samples.

What we want from a sample is a reasonable representation of the population, and this is why we take samples. **We take samples in order to estimate the quality of the population from the quality of the sample.**

The question then becomes, why not measure the entire population and then there will be no need to estimate at all? There are a number of answers to this question, and one or more may apply in a particular case.

5-1.1   One Hundred Percent Inspection

One hundred percent inspection generally turns out in practice to be somewhat less than 100%, particularly where the testing procedure is of a monotonous repetitive nature. Monotonous tasks have a way of making us behave in an automatic manner, and when we develop this automaticity, as the industrial engineers call it, we tend to stop thinking about what we are doing. Under these circumstances, if 95% of the items have to go in one bin and 5% in another, there is a chance that some of the 5% are going to end up being "automatically" dropped in the bin where 95% of our movements are directed.

The result of this is that **it is generally accepted that only about 85% to 95% of the defective items are removed by 100% inspection.** Unless extreme precision or human life is involved, we are therefore just as well to use a system of sampling and a known confidence level.

5-1.2   Destruction of the Product

Another reason is that **conducting the test may destroy the product.** If we scoop out a liquid sample from a container of some kind, we have only minutely reduced the volume and we can analyze this sample without affecting the product. On the other hand, if we have to drill a hole in an item in order to get drillings for analysis, we have probably destroyed the unit, and we can obviously not do this to all our production.

Strength tests where a material is stressed to destruction obviously destroy the product, but even a hardness test on a machined surface can sometimes render it unsuitable for its intended purpose. Ascertaining the expected life of electric light bulbs or the wear resistance of different combinations of material are all in the same category. The product is destroyed during testing, and a sample must therefore be used to estimate the nature of the population as a whole.

5-1.3   Cost of Testing

Cost can be another factor in the decision to take samples rather than test the entire production. The more complex the inspection or testing procedure, and the more highly skilled the personnel conducting the tests, the more costly they are likely to be.

Whether the inspection costs are included in the overhead charges or are a direct cost applied to specific jobs is immaterial; they are manufacturing costs which must be born by the organization, but which may be minimized by intelligent sampling.

5-1.4   Testing Time

The **time involved in conducting the test** can be another factor influencing the amount of testing that can be practicable. If items can be tested as quickly as they are produced, there might be an argument in favor of attempting 100% inspection; but if it takes half an hour to test 5 pounds of material and during that half hour 5 tons of the material pass along a conveyor belt, then there would be a strong argument in favor of only taking samples. It would be a rare operation indeed where production could be shut down while waiting on the test results.

5-1.5   Flow of Material

When material passes along a pipe or a conveyor into a vat or holding vessel where thorough mixing takes place, one test when the vat is filled can fairly represent that unit of production. When no mixing vessel exists however, and the material continues down the line to another process, then some type of sampling procedure will have to be devised which will allow an estimate to be made of the properties of the entire production. So, apart from the time it takes to conduct the testing procedure, where it is not possible to differentiate among discrete batches of product, sampling becomes a necessity.

5-2   SAMPLING PROCEDURES

Whatever procedure we use, it must be such that we do not take biased samples. We have seen that the top layer in a basket of apples may be biased in the direction of higher quality, and this can also happen with industrial samples. Industrial samples may also be biased on the lower side of quality.

5-2.1   Systematic Sampling

There are so many sources or causes of biased samples that it would not be possible to cover every case in every industry, but one of the most common arises from the taking of systematic samples. **System-**

atic samples are samples taken at some kind of regular interval. The inspector may check every fifth or every tenth item, for example, or the technician may test the material at regular half-hour intervals. Operators can become very skilled at knowing when the next item is going to be lifted from the conveyor and checked by the inspector and, of course, that item gets a little bit of extra attention. In very large plants where there are a number of inspectors on the one line, this may not be a factor as there may be too many inspectors to watch, but it can crop up in medium- to small-sized operations. Anyone can watch a clock, however, and it is not too difficult for an operator to prepare for the taking of each sample.

Another source of bias with systematic sampling can occur when the operation is of a cyclical nature, and the length of the cycle corresponds with the interval of time between samples. If a machine processes a large piece of raw material into a number of small items, and each time a new piece of raw material is loaded adjustments have to be made before the product is correctly to size, then samples taken at the start of each cycle will indicate variations which do not take place during the remainder of the run. Similarly, some processes have a start-up adjustment phase, a running phase, and a shut-down adjustment phase. Samples taken systematically at only the start, middle, **or** end of each run could indicate conditions which are much better or much worse than the true overall conditions which exist throughout the day.

Systematic sampling must not be completely condemned, however, as it permits uniform scheduling of the work of the technicians or inspectors. Where these people do not have other duties which could fit into irregular schedules, systematic sampling permits most effective use of their time.

If we are going to use systematic sampling because of its convenience, we can add a technique which will eliminate the risk of drawing samples from the same phase of each cycle and will reduce to some extent the ability of some of the operators to figure out the inspection schedule. This procedure consists of taking the **first** sample each day or each half-shift at a **random time** and all samples thereafter in a regular systematic manner. For this method to be effective that first time must be truly random. It is not good enough to say that today the first sample will be taken before we have a coffee from the machine, and tomorrow we will wait until after finishing that first cup of coffee. **To be truly random, each minute in the hour should have an equal opportunity of being selected.**

One method of accomplishing this is to write the numbers 1 to

60 on pieces of paper and to draw one from the lot today to obtain **the minutes after starting time for the first sample tomorrow.** If 60 minutes seems too long a time to randomize, then perhaps it could be confined to the first 30 minutes of the day.

To avoid the drawing of numbers from a hat, random time tables can be used. These are tables of columns of preselected random times, and by working down any one column and then moving to another column, sample starting times will be obtained which will be truly random. No one will be able to guess when tomorrow's first sample will be taken. Appendix 2 is an example of such a table. To use the table we might start in column 1 and take our sample on the first day 26 minutes after starting time. On succeeding days it would be taken at 54, 42, 22, 17, and 58 minutes after starting time, and so on down the column. After using all possible times from one column, we then select times from another column, which may be taken in sequence or may itself be selected in a random manner.

5-2.2   Random Sampling

If we can have an advantage in randomizing the first sample, surely it would be an even greater advantage to randomize all the samples. Where the work of the inspectors can be scheduled to take care of wide variations in the frequency of sampling, complete random sampling will eliminate any chance of operators predicting when samples will be drawn, as well as obtain a correct proportion of start-up and shut-down samples, **in the long run.**

To be truly random, each item or unit of production should have an equal opportunity of being selected. To make the selection of random times more convenient for complete random sampling, the times in Appendix 2 have been arranged in sequence, and these form Appendix 3. The times in each column are in sequence, and each column can represent a different hour from starting time. Work from left to right and top to bottom, then right to left and bottom to top, then every odd-numbered column, then every even-numbered column, and then any combination or variation of any of these or other systems..By doing this, no two days in any week and no two weeks in any month should have the same schedule of sampling times.

Quality control is not only concerned with work in process; it is also concerned with checking incoming parts and raw materials, and these should also be sampled in a random manner so as to avoid bias. Items arriving in crates or tote boxes and raw materials piled in the yard can all be randomly sampled with the aid of random number tables, as shown in Appendix 4.

With boxed material or items, we can draw up a grid similar to that shown in Figure 5-1, with the number of layers being dependent on the approximate depth occupied by a single item and the number of subdivisions in each layer being dependent on the approximate area occupied by one item. With granular materials the depth can simply be numbered off in inches (or centimeters) and the horizontal squares made to any size convenient for digging out an adequate size of sample. The next step is to go to the table of random numbers and choose two digits from a column to represent the horizontal grid number and two digits to represent the depth. Then, if only one sample is to be taken from each box, we progress down the first column, discarding impossible combinations, until we arrive at the first combination which meets our sampling requirements. For the next box, we continue down the first column and then move over to the next, and so on. For example, if we let the first two digits represent the grid and the third represent the level, the first random sample to meet the requirements of Figure 5-1 is fifth from the top of column 1. That is, it will be taken from grid position 19 at a depth of layer 2. When more than one sample is to be taken from a box, it is necessary to preselect all random positions first, because the last one drawn from the table could turn out to be the first one to be drawn from the box. For example, if we desire to take ten samples from a box to which Figure 5-1 would apply, and we choose to have the first two digits represent grid number and the third to represent

Figure 5–1   Sampling Grid for Boxed Items

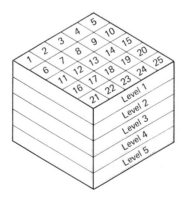

level number, then the first ten possible number combinations would be:

Grid Number	Level	Sequence in Table	Sequence Of Sampling
19	2	1	2
1	8	2	6
12	2	3	2
22	1	4	1
3	5	5	5
4	8	6	6
15	4	7	4
17	4	8	4
23	4	9	4
1	3	10	3

Notice that the first drawn from the table will be the second sample drawn from the box, and the fourth sample drawn from the table will be the first sample drawn from the box. (*Note:* Where more than one sample has to be drawn from one level, they have been given the same sequence number.) Preplanning is therefore essential.

In the case of sampling from raw material piled in a yard, a similar procedure can be used except that the grid pattern will have to conform to the shape of the pile of material. There is always a strong tendency on the part of those taking samples from bulk storage piles to draw from the bottom of the pile for the simple reason of convenience. This can cause biased sampling where lump materials are concerned, as the strongest material tends to break down the least and hence forms the largest lumps. These large lumps also have a tendency to roll to the bottom of the pile. The use of a grid pattern and random-number tables together with providing adequate means of access to various heights in the pile will give randomly selected, unbiased samples.

5-3   HOMOGENEOUS SAMPLES

In Chapter 1 we noted how words like "quality" and "quality control" can mean different things in different industries, and the same is true of the word "sample." In processing industries a jar of liquid or a lump of material sent to the laboratory for analysis is known as "a sample," while in the mass-production field a number of items taken from a batch is known as "a sample." In the latter case, we might have 50 items taken from a batch for inspection or measurement, and that 50 would be known as the sample. If we then repeated this procedure 20 times in a shift, we would have inspected 20 times 50 or 1,000 items. Notice that we have not taken 1,000 samples; we have taken 20 samples of size 50. It is in this connotation that the word "sample" is most often used in quality control.

If a sample, then, consists of a number of measurements from individual items, it is most important that that sample be homogeneous. That is, the items in each sample must all come from the same universe (or population). This sounds like a reasonable statement to make but problems arise when a number of processes which are **ostensibly the same** are producing **ostensibly the same item,** but from different process capabilities.

Machines and processes have a way of wearing out or going out of adjustment at different rates, and operators have a way of exercising various degrees of skill. Putting these together, our multiple sources of a single product may prove to be multiple universes of that product. If random sampling is being used, the product from each machine will be sampled proportionately, **in the long run,** and these samples may even be normally distributed. If the coefficient of variation is large, however, compared to that for other similar quality characteristics in the same plant, then the processes should be examined individually to determine if the samples are indeed homogeneous. It is not uncommon to find that either the standard deviations are close and the means vary or that the means are close and the standard deviations vary. Zero errors in machine settings can cause the former, and varying amounts of play in moving parts can cause the latter.

Collecting samples by individual machines or processes may seem like an expensive business to some managers, but it can pay dividends when it signals the need to take a particular machine out of service for major repairs. It can also indicate the machines to use **(at no extra cost)** when a tight specification has been accepted. A customer's specification may be narrower than the overall process capability, but as wide as or wider than that of those machines which are in best condition. Obviously, the tight-specification products should be confined to those machines with the narrowest process capabilities. Aiming for homogeneous samples can therefore result in other indirect manufacturing advantages.

A homogeneous sample in the quality-control sense must not

be confused with a homogeneous sample in the process industry sense. The former is desirable, the latter may not be.

Where product is passing along a pipe or conveyor, it may be possible to bleed off or plow off a small fraction of the material on a continuous basis. If this material is collected and mixed, then a test conducted on it will give an **average** condition for the production over a specific period of time. The sample will indeed be homogeneous, but it will not give a true indication of the variations which take place in the process. A sample for analysis or test, drawn from a process, must indeed be homogeneous in the sense of being well mixed or the test results may be ridiculous. Homogeneity achieved by mixing material from different stages in the process, however, will only mask the true variation taking place. Random or random-systematic testing will indicate the true amount of process variation, **in the long run.** It is never a good idea to fool yourself, or anyone else, into thinking that a process has a narrower process capability than is in fact the case.

5-4   THE CENTRAL LIMIT THEOREM

We stated earlier that we take samples to estimate the quality of the population from the quality of the samples, and in Table 5-1 we have an example where we have collected the variable measurements in samples of three. The values in each sample are then added and their totals appear in the $\sum x$ column. Next this total is divided by the number of items in the sample (in this case, 3) and the mean recorded in the $\bar{x}$ column. Thirty-six samples were collected and their distribution is shown graphically by the solid line in Figure 5-2. This line varies up and down in a random manner and ranges from a low of 5.12 to a high of 6.01, compared to a low of 4.75 and a high of 6.57 for the individual items. That is, the range in values decreased from 1.82 for the individual values to 0.89 for the means.

If accumulating the values in sets of three can produce this amount of evening out of the variations, it would be of interest to see what happens if we accumulate all the samples progressively from start to finish. The sample totals have, therefore, been added to each other progressively down the column headed Cumulative Total. The cumulative mean, recorded in the last column, is simply the cumulative total divided by the total number of individual results up to that point.

Table 5-1 CUMULATIVE MEAN OF SAMPLES: SAMPLE SIZE = 3

Sample Number	Individual Values x 1	2	3	Sample Total $\sum x$	Sample Mean $\bar{x}$	Cumulative Total	Cumulative Mean
1	6.57	5.59	5.87	18.03	6.01	18.03	6.01
2	5.59	5.87	5.45	16.91	5.64	34.94	5.82
3	4.89	5.17	5.73	15.79	5.26	50.73	5.64
4	5.73	5.73	4.89	16.35	5.45	67.08	5.59
5	5.73	5.45	5.45	16.63	5.54	83.71	5.58
6	5.45	5.03	5.45	15.93	5.31	99.64	5.54
7	5.31	5.03	5.59	15.93	5.31	115.57	5.50
8	5.45	4.89	5.03	15.37	5.12	130.94	5.46
9	5.45	6.01	5.31	16.77	5.59	147.71	5.47
10	5.03	5.31	5.17	15.51	5.17	163.22	5.44
11	5.59	5.87	6.01	17.47	5.82	180.69	5.48
12	5.59	5.59	5.03	16.21	5.40	196.90	5.47
13	6.15	5.73	5.59	17.47	5.82	214.37	5.50
14	5.45	5.59	5.03	16.07	5.36	230.44	5.49
15	5.87	5.45	5.59	16.91	5.64	247.35	5.50
16	5.45	5.17	5.31	15.93	5.31	263.28	5.49
17	5.31	5.31	5.59	16.21	5.40	279.49	5.48
18	5.45	5.31	5.31	16.07	5.36	295.56	5.47
19	5.31	5.73	5.87	16.91	5.64	312.47	5.48
20	5.45	5.45	5.17	16.07	5.36	328.54	5.48
21	5.73	4.75	6.01	16.49	5.50	345.03	5.48
22	5.17	6.01	5.31	16.49	5.50	361.52	5.48
23	5.17	5.17	5.45	15.79	5.26	377.31	5.47
24	5.31	5.59	5.59	16.49	5.50	393.80	5.47
25	5.45	5.59	5.87	16.91	5.64	410.71	5.48
26	5.31	5.59	5.73	16.63	5.54	427.34	5.48
27	6.01	5.87	5.45	17.33	5.78	444.67	5.49
28	5.73	5.59	5.73	17.05	5.68	461.72	5.50
29	5.31	5.59	5.73	16.63	5.54	478.35	5.50
30	5.45	5.59	5.73	16.77	5.59	495.12	5.50
31	5.17	6.15	5.73	17.05	5.68	512.17	5.51
32	5.59	5.17	5.73	16.49	5.50	528.66	5.51
33	5.31	5.45	5.31	16.07	5.36	544.73	5.50
34	5.73	4.89	5.17	15.79	5.26	560.52	5.50
35	5.45	5.17	5.87	16.49	5.50	577.01	5.50
36	5.03	5.45	5.45	15.93	5.31	592.94	5.49

The broken line in Figure 5-2 indicates the progression of the cumulative mean from start to finish, and not only are the extreme variations evened out, but a point seems to be reached where the addition of another sample total makes little difference to the cumulative mean. **After** sample 10 the mean seems to stabilize at between 5.47 and 5.51. It would therefore be reasonable to assume that additional samples would have a similar minor effect and that, although the overall mean is 5.49, the mean for the **population** will likely be found within this range of from 5.47 to 5.51.

If we now retabulate the values in samples of six, retaining the same sequence as in Table 5-1, we obtain a reduced number of samples and a reduced range in values. Table 5-2 shows the revised values with a range of from 5.22 to 5.82 (or only 0.60), and Figure 5-3 shows the progression of the cumulative mean. In this case, it levels off in the 5.47 to 5.51 range **after** sample 5.

This procedure was repeated for samples of nine values, again carefully retaining the same sequence of results. In the case of size nine, the cumulative mean stabilized in the 5.47 to 5.51 range **after** the second sample.

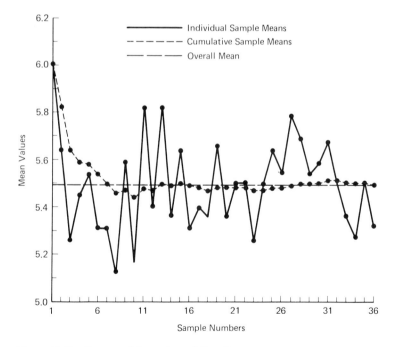

Figure 5-2   Means of Samples of Size 3

Table 5-2   CUMULATIVE MEAN OF SAMPLES: SAMPLE SIZE = 6

Sample Number	x						Sample Total $\sum x$	Sample Mean $\bar{x}$	Cumulative Mean
	1	2	3	4	5	6			
1	6.57	5.59	5.87	5.59	5.87	5.45	34.94	5.82	5.82
2	4.89	5.17	5.73	5.73	5.73	4.89	32.14	5.36	5.59
3	5.73	5.45	5.45	5.45	5.03	5.45	32.56	5.43	5.54
4	5.31	5.03	5.59	5.45	4.89	5.03	31.30	5.22	5.46
5	5.45	6.01	5.31	5.03	5.31	5.17	32.28	5.38	5.44
6	5.59	5.87	6.01	5.59	5.59	5.03	33.68	5.61	5.47
7	6.15	5.73	5.59	5.45	5.59	5.03	33.54	5.59	5.49
8	5.87	5.45	5.59	5.45	5.17	5.31	32.84	5.47	5.49
9	5.31	5.31	5.59	5.45	5.31	5.31	32.28	5.38	5.47
.0	5.31	5.73	5.87	5.45	5.45	5.17	32.98	5.50	5.48
11	5.73	4.75	6.01	5.17	6.01	5.31	32.98	5.50	5.48
12	5.17	5.17	5.45	5.31	5.59	5.59	32.28	5.38	
13	5.45	5.59	5.87	5.31	5.59	5.73	33.54	5.59	5.48
14	6.01	5.87	5.45	5.73	5.59	5.73	34.38	5.73	5.50
15	5.31	5.59	5.73	5.45	5.59	5.73	33.40	5.57	5.50
16	5.17	6.15	5.73	5.59	5.17	5.73	33.54	5.59	5.51
17	5.31	5.45	5.31	5.73	4.89	5.17	31.86	5.31	5.50
18	5.45	5.17	5.87	5.03	5.45	5.45	32.42	5.40	5.49

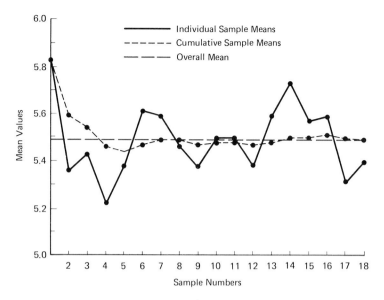

Figure 5–3 Means of Samples of Size 6

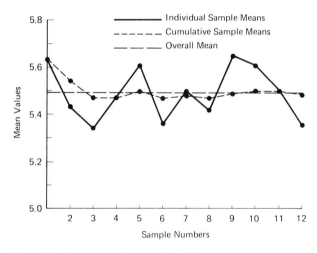

Figure 5–4 Means of Samples of Size 9

Table 5-3 CUMULATIVE MEAN OF SAMPLES: SAMPLE SIZE = 9

Sample Number	x 1	2	3	4	5	6	7	8	9	Sample Total $\sum x$	Sample Mean $\bar{x}$	Cumulative Mean
1	6.57	5.59	5.87	5.59	5.87	5.45	4.89	5.17	5.73	50.73	5.64	5.64
2	5.73	5.73	4.89	5.73	5.45	5.45	5.45	5.03	5.45	48.91	5.43	5.54
3	5.31	5.03	5.59	5.45	4.89	5.03	5.45	6.01	5.31	48.07	5.34	5.47
4	5.03	5.31	5.17	5.59	5.87	6.01	5.59	5.59	5.03	49.19	5.47	5.47
5	6.15	5.73	5.59	5.45	5.59	5.03	5.87	5.45	5.59	50.45	5.61	5.50
6	5.45	5.17	5.31	5.31	5.31	5.59	5.45	5.31	5.31	48.21	5.36	5.47
7	5.31	5.73	5.87	5.45	5.45	5.17	5.73	4.75	6.01	49.47	5.50	5.48
8	5.17	6.01	5.31	5.17	5.17	5.45	5.31	5.59	5.59	48.77	5.42	5.47
9	5.45	5.59	5.87	5.31	5.59	5.73	6.01	5.87	5.45	50.87	5.65	5.49
10	5.73	5.59	5.73	5.31	5.59	5.73	5.45	5.59	5.73	50.45	5.61	5.50
11	5.17	6.15	5.73	5.59	5.17	5.73	5.31	5.45	5.31	49.61	5.51	5.50
12	5.73	4.89	5.17	5.45	5.17	5.87	5.03	5.45	5.45	48.21	5.36	5.49

To partly summarize, we found that

Sample size 3   stabilized after sample 10 or 30 items.
Sample size 6   stabilized after sample 5 or 30 items.
Sample size 9   stabilized after sample 2 or 18 items.

In other words, in most cases it took no more than 30 items in our example to arrive at a condition where the cumulative mean varied by only ±0.02 from the overall mean (i.e., ±0.4% of the overall mean). In none of the cases could we say that a stable condition had finally been reached, but as more and more samples are taken this will eventually happen, and the cumulative mean will level off at the population mean. As leveling off started sooner with the largest samples, it is reasonable to assume that the population mean would also be arrived at sooner with the use of larger samples.

Another feature which we noted was the reduction in the range of values as we progressed to larger samples.

	Minimum	Maximum	Range
Individual values	4.75	6.57	1.82
Sample size 3	5.12	6.01	0.89
Sample size 6	5.22	5.82	0.60
Sample size 9	5.34	5.65	0.31

So as we took larger and larger samples, there was a tendency for the variation from mean to mean to become progressively less and less.

The standard deviation is the measure of dispersion which we have used for individual results and, as we now see that there is also dispersion among means, we use it also here. There is one difference, however; we call it by a different name. We call it the *standard error of the means*. The different name is simply to avoid confusion with population parameters, for in every other way it is exactly the same as a standard deviation.

With the range in values tending to decrease as we progress to larger and larger samples, it would seem reasonable to expect that this would also be true for the standard errors of the means, and this is in fact the case.

Individual Values	Standard Deviation	0.31
Sample size 3	Standard error of the means	0.20
Sample size 6	Standard error of the means	0.15
Sample size 9	Standard error of the means	0.11

Figure 5-5 shows what the normal curves look like for three of these cases, the individual values, samples of three, and samples of nine. It can clearly be seen from this illustration how dramatically the distribution of values decreases when we deal with means rather than individual values. It also shows why the larger samples arrive at the true mean more quickly; there is simply less scope for variation.

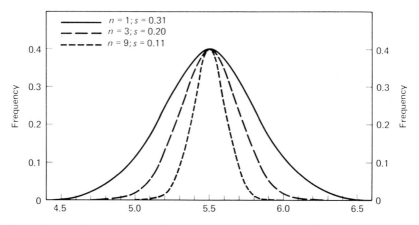

Figure 5–5 Change in Distribution with Change in Sample Size

The central limit theorem summarizes all the foregoing and adds to it. It is a very important theorem in statistical quality-control work and should be thoroughly studied. **The central limit theorem states that if we draw samples of size *n* from a population with a mean μ and a standard deviation σ, then as *n* increases in size the distribution of sample means approaches a normal distribution with a mean μ and a standard error of the means of $\sigma/\sqrt{n}$.**

First, this tells us that, even if the individual values are not normally distributed, the distribution of the means will tend to be normally distributed, and the larger the sample size the greater this tendency will be. It also tells us that the mean of the means $(\bar{\bar{x}})$ will be the same as the mean of the population (μ), in the long run, but this is something that we already guessed from observing cumulative means.

The aspect which we could not have guessed at is the mathematical relationship between the standard deviation and the standard error of the means.

$$\text{Standard error of the means} = \frac{\text{standard deviation of the population}}{\sqrt{\text{sample size}}}$$

In symbols, this is written

$$\sigma_{\bar{x}} = \frac{\sigma}{\sqrt{n}}$$

Stated in this manner, we can find the standard error of the means for a given sample size if we know the standard deviation for the population. However, we have already stated that the purpose of taking samples is to estimate the quality of the population from the quality of the samples, so we are most likely to use this formula with standard deviation stated as the unknown. That is;

$$\sigma = \sigma_{\bar{x}} \sqrt{n}$$

We can now use this formula to estimate the standard deviation from the information we have for our four different sample sizes.

Sample size 3:   Estimate of standard deviation $= 0.20 \sqrt{3} = 0.35$

Sample size 6:   Estimate of standard deviation $= 0.15 \sqrt{6} = 0.37$

Sample size 9:   Estimate of standard deviation $= 0.11 \sqrt{9} = 0.33$

These do not look like very good estimates, considering the fact that the individual values were calculated to have a standard deviation of 0.316. The problem is due largely to the very small number of values on which the standard errors of the mean were based. We would absolutely never base any practical decisions on such a small amount of data. However, it is also true that it is more accurate to estimate standard deviation from the variation **within** the samples rather than **between** the samples, and we will deal with this in Chapter 6.

QUESTIONS AND PROBLEMS

---

1. Describe what is meant by a "biased" sample.

2. What is the purpose of taking samples?

3. Describe why 100% inspection generally does not result in the removal of 100% of the defective items when large numbers are being inspected.

4. Describe two reasons why it may be desirable or essential to take samples rather than to inspect or test all the product.

5. Describe an advantage and a disadvantage to the use of systematic sampling procedures.

6. What is the essential characteristic of any random-sampling procedure?

7. Items to be inspected are contained in boxes measuring 2 ft by 2 ft by 2 ft. Each item is approximately 4 in. in diameter, and three items are to be checked from each box. Draw up a random sampling plan for the first ten boxes in a series, using the table in Appendix 4.

8. Describe what is meant by a "homogeneous sample" when used in the context of quality control.

9. If we were to take a number of series of samples of different sizes from the same population of values, what difference or differences would we expect to find associated with the means of these samples?

10. State the central limit theorem.

6

Average and Range: The $\bar{x}$-R Chart

In Chapter 4 we defined process capability as being the range of three standard deviations on either side of the mean. These limits were chosen because they are at the start of the tailing off of the normal curve and, by chance alone, will include 99.73% of the values. In other words, there is only one chance in 370 of a result falling **either above or below** these limits by chance alone.

These same limits are used to define the range within which we expect to find the mean values, and the mean of the means plus and minus three standard errors of the mean will include 99.73% of all mean values, **in the long run.** The limits of this range we call the *control limits*, and these are given as follows:

$$\mathrm{UCL}_{\bar{x}} = \bar{\bar{x}} + 3\sigma_{\bar{x}}$$

$$\mathrm{LCL}_{\bar{x}} = \bar{\bar{x}} - 3\sigma_{\bar{x}}$$

where $\mathrm{UCL}_{\bar{x}}$ = upper control limit for means
$\mathrm{LCL}_{\bar{x}}$ = lower control limit for means
$\bar{\bar{x}}$ = mean of the means
$\sigma_{\bar{x}}$ = standard error of the means

Note: It is time consuming to calculate the cumulative mean, or the mean of all the x values, so we simply find the sum of all the means $(\Sigma\bar{x})$ and divide by the number of samples (N); i.e., $\bar{\bar{x}} = \Sigma \bar{x}/N$.

A word of caution is necessary here. It is only permissible to average means when they are from samples of equal size. We cannot add the mean for a sample of 100 to the mean of a sample of 5 and divide by 2 and expect to get the overall mean. For example,

$$
\begin{array}{llll}
\text{Sample size} = 100 & & \text{Mean} = 10 \\
\text{Sample size} = \underline{5} & & \text{Mean} = \underline{2} \\
\qquad\text{Total} \quad 105 & & \qquad\text{Total} \quad 12
\end{array}
$$

The mean of the 105 items is not $12/2 = 6$; it is found by weighting each value. Thus

$$
\begin{array}{ll}
100 \times 10 = 1{,}000 \\
5 \times 2 = \underline{10} \\
\quad\text{Total} \quad 1{,}010
\end{array}
$$

$$
\text{Mean} = \frac{1{,}010}{105}
$$

$$
= 9.6
$$

To avoid the weighting calculation and other problems of interpretation of results, **we must therefore use samples of equal size for any particular variable being studied.**

Because of the fact that the means tend to be normally distributed even if the population is not, we can rely on the means to indicate when a normal or an abnormal condition exists. When variations occur within $\pm3\sigma_{\bar{x}}$, we say that they are produced by chance causes. **Chance causes are produced by the sources of variation** (described in Section 1-5) **and hence can never be entirely eliminated as they are related to all aspects of the process involved.**

When results fall outside the $\pm3\sigma_{\bar{x}}$ limits, we say that they were produced by assignable causes. By this we mean that we can assign or relate a specific cause to a specific variation. Results can fall outside the control limits by chance alone, but this chance is so slight that for most practical purposes it can be ignored. **Assignable causes** are specific events or conditions which produce nonnormal variation in the process.

The identification of assignable causes is one of the most important functions of the quality-control department and when doing so each of the sources of variation must be examined. For example;

1. **Raw Material:** Has the specification been changed or has the wrong material been used?

2. **Operator:** Is the operator fully trained? Does he or she have a hangover? Is the operator overtired through working excessive overtime? Does the operator have a current grievance pending?

3. **Process:** Are automatic controls operating correctly? Has the correct temperature or pressure been used? Are all tools or dies in correct condition?

4. **Method of Measurement:** Are standards available for checking the instrumentation? Have all measuring devices been checked for errors? Are the devices being used correctly?

These are only examples of the kinds of questions which must be asked and answered in the search for assignable causes, and of course each specific process should have its own list of appropriate questions.

6-2 RANGE AND SAMPLE SIZE

In Chapter 5, we saw that as we took larger samples we needed fewer of them to arrive at a stable mean and that there tended to be less variation from mean to mean, but we did not look at the variation **within** each sample. Just as mean can vary by chance from sample to sample, so also can the standard deviation within each sample. Just as an assignable cause can alter the mean or the mean of the means, so also can an assignable cause alter the standard deviation within the samples and within the population. In other words, a factor which affects the mean will not necessarily affect the standard deviation, and a factor which affects the standard deviation will not necessarily affect the mean.

Both of these sample statistics are important to us in quality control, but standard deviation is not convenient to use because of the calculations involved. **Instead we use the range of values within each sample or subgroup, as an immediate measure of the variation taking place and the mean of all the ranges to determine the standard error of the means.**

$$\text{Range} = \text{maximum value} - \text{minimum value}$$

The mean of the ranges is found from the formula:

$$\overline{R} = \frac{\Sigma R}{n}$$

where $\overline{R}$ = mean of the sample ranges
ΣR = sum of the sample ranges
n = number of samples

The data from Table 5-1 have been arranged in Table 6-1 in the manner which is typical of $\overline{x} - R$ tabulations. The statistics obtained from Table 6-1 are

$$\overline{\overline{x}} = \frac{\Sigma \overline{x}}{n} = \frac{157.65}{36} = 5.49$$

$$\overline{R} = \frac{\Sigma R}{n} = \frac{18.48}{36} = 0.51$$

Similarly, Tables 5-2 and 5-3 have been converted into Tables 6-2 and 6-3, respectively, giving the following results:

Sample Size	$\overline{\overline{x}}$	$\overline{R}$
3	5.490	0.513
6	5.491	0.778
9	5.492	0.945

Table 6-1   TABLE OF MEAN AND RANGE: SUBGROUP SIZE = 3

Subgroup Number	x 1	x 2	x 3	Σx	$\bar{x}$	R
1	6.57	5.59	5.87	18.03	6.01	0.98
2	5.59	5.87	5.45	16.91	5.64	0.42
3	4.89	5.17	5.73	15.79	5.26	0.84
4	5.73	5.73	4.89	16.35	5.45	0.84
5	5.73	5.45	5.45	16.63	5.54	0.28
6	5.45	5.03	5.45	15.93	5.31	0.42
7	5.31	5.03	5.59	15.93	5.31	0.56
8	5.45	4.89	5.03	15.37	5.12	0.56
9	5.45	6.01	5.31	16.77	5.59	0.70
10	5.03	5.31	5.17	15.51	5.17	0.28
11	5.59	5.87	6.01	17.47	5.82	0.42
12	5.59	5.59	5.03	16.21	5.40	0.56
13	6.15	5.73	5.59	17.47	5.82	0.56
14	5.45	5.59	5.03	16.07	5.36	0.56
15	5.87	5.45	5.59	16.91	5.64	0.42
16	5.45	5.17	5.31	15.93	5.31	0.28
17	5.31	5.31	5.59	16.21	5.40	0.28
18	5.45	5.31	5.31	16.07	5.36	0.14
19	5.31	5.73	5.87	16.91	5.64	0.56
20	5.45	5.45	5.17	16.07	5.36	0.28
21	5.73	4.75	6.01	16.49	5.50	1.26
22	5.17	6.01	5.31	16.49	5.50	0.84
23	5.17	5.17	5.45	15.79	5.26	0.28
24	5.31	5.59	5.59	16.49	5.50	0.28
25	5.45	5.59	5.87	16.91	5.64	0.42
26	5.31	5.59	5.73	16.63	5.54	0.42
27	6.01	5.87	5.45	17.33	5.78	0.56
28	5.73	5.59	5.73	17.05	5.68	0.14
29	5.31	5.59	5.73	16.63	5.54	0.42
30	5.45	5.59	5.73	16.77	5.59	0.28
31	5.17	6.15	5.73	17.05	5.68	0.98
32	5.59	5.17	5.73	16.49	5.50	0.56
33	5.31	5.45	5.31	16.07	5.36	0.14
34	5.73	4.89	5.17	15.79	5.26	0.84
35	5.45	5.17	5.87	16.49	5.50	0.70
36	5.03	5.45	5.45	15.93	5.31	0.42
					157.65	18.48

Table 6-2 TABLE OF MEAN AND RANGE: SUBGROUP SIZE = 6

Subgroup Number	x 1	2	3	4	5	6	Σx	x̄	R
1	6.57	5.59	5.87	5.59	5.87	5.45	34.94	5.82	1.12
2	4.89	5.17	5.73	5.73	5.73	4.89	32.14	5.36	0.84
3	5.73	5.45	5.45	5.45	5.03	5.45	32.56	5.43	0.70
4	5.31	5.03	5.59	5.45	4.89	5.03	31.30	5.22	0.70
5	5.45	6.01	5.31	5.03	5.31	5.17	32.28	5.38	0.98
6	5.59	5.87	6.01	5.59	5.59	5.03	33.68	5.61	0.98
7	6.15	5.73	5.59	5.45	5.59	5.03	33.54	5.59	1.12
8	5.87	5.45	5.59	5.45	5.17	5.31	32.84	5.47	0.70
9	5.31	5.31	5.59	5.45	5.31	5.31	32.28	5.38	0.28
10	5.31	5.73	5.87	5.45	5.45	5.17	32.98	5.50	0.70
11	5.73	4.75	6.01	5.17	6.01	5.31	32.98	5.50	1.26
12	5.17	5.17	5.45	5.31	5.59	5.59	32.28	5.38	0.42
13	5.45	5.59	5.87	5.31	5.59	5.73	33.54	5.59	0.56
14	6.01	5.87	5.45	5.73	5.59	5.73	34.38	5.73	0.56
15	5.31	5.59	5.73	5.45	5.59	5.73	33.40	5.57	0.42
16	5.17	6.15	5.73	5.59	5.17	5.73	33.54	5.59	0.98
17	5.31	5.45	5.31	5.73	4.89	5.17	31.86	5.31	0.84
18	5.45	5.17	5.87	5.03	5.45	5.45	32.42	5.40	0.84
								58.83	14.00

Table 6-3 TABLE OF MEAN AND RANGE: SUBGROUP SIZE = 9

Sample Number	x									Σx	$\bar{x}$	R
	1	2	3	4	5	6	7	8	9			
1	6.57	5.59	5.87	5.59	5.87	5.45	4.89	5.17	5.73	50.73	5.64	1.68
2	5.73	5.73	4.89	5.73	5.45	5.45	5.45	5.03	5.45	48.91	5.43	0.84
3	5.31	5.03	5.59	5.45	4.89	5.03	5.45	6.01	5.31	48.07	5.34	1.12
4	5.03	5.31	5.17	5.59	5.87	6.01	5.59	5.59	5.03	49.19	5.47	0.98
5	6.15	5.73	5.59	5.45	5.59	5.03	5.87	5.45	5.59	50.45	5.61	1.12
6	5.45	5.17	5.31	5.31	5.31	5.59	5.45	5.31	5.31	48.21	5.36	0.42
7	5.31	5.73	5.87	5.45	5.45	5.17	5.73	4.75	6.01	49.47	5.50	1.26
8	5.17	6.01	5.31	5.17	5.17	5.45	5.31	5.59	5.59	48.77	5.42	0.84
9	5.45	5.59	5.87	5.31	5.59	5.73	6.01	5.87	5.45	50.87	5.65	0.70
10	5.73	5.59	5.73	5.31	5.59	5.73	5.45	5.59	5.73	50.45	5.61	0.42
11	5.17	6.15	5.73	5.59	5.17	5.73	5.31	5.45	5.31	49.61	5.51	0.98
12	5.73	4.89	5.17	5.45	5.17	5.87	5.03	5.45	5.45	48.21	5.36	0.98
											65.90	11.34

So we find that as the sample size increases and we bite off a larger portion of the population, that sample includes more of the extreme values in the population and the mean range consequently increases. In fact, Figure 6-1 shows that the results for our variable fall close to a straight line when plotted on semilogarithmic graph paper.

The 6σ process capability of our set of 108 individual values was 1.90, and it is interesting to note that if we extrapolate our graph (or substitute 1.9 for $\overline{R}$ in the equation), we obtain a sample size of about 91 at an $\overline{R}$ value of 1.9. In other words, the equation tells us that, if we want our sampling plan to encompass the expected maximum range of values, the samples will have to be almost the same size as the original set of values **in this case.**

In summary, then, larger samples approach the population

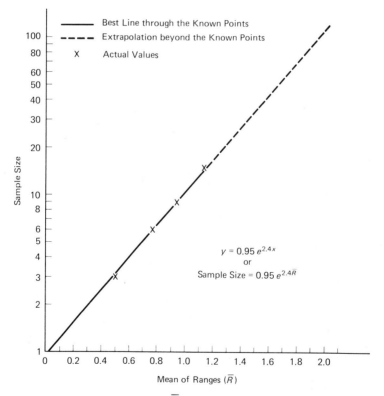

Figure 6–1   Sample size and $\overline{R}$ (See Appendix 6 for correlation information)

mean more quickly, have lower variations from mean to mean, but higher variations within the samples. As one increases the other decreases, so as long as we keep track of both we are unlikely to delude ourselves with false ideas about the amount of variation in the population.

6–3   CALCULATION OF CONTROL LIMITS
FOR MEAN FROM $\bar{R}$

We have already seen that the control limits for mean are set at $\pm3\sigma_{\bar{x}}$, but in Chapter 5 we saw that calculation of $\sigma_{\bar{x}}$ directly from the sample means was lacking in accuracy. Fortunately, there is a method of arriving at control limits which eliminates the necessity to calculate the standard error of the means and, instead, obtains the values directly from $\bar{R}$ and a predetermined constant. The A_2 values in Appendix 5 give the control limits using the formulas

$$\mathrm{UCL}_{\bar{x}} = \bar{\bar{x}} + A_2\bar{R}$$

$$\mathrm{LCL}_{\bar{x}} = \bar{\bar{x}} - A_2\bar{R}$$

Tabulating the information on our examples gives the following:

Sample Size	A_2	$\bar{R}$	$A_2\bar{R}$	$\mathrm{UCL}_{\bar{x}}$	$\mathrm{LCL}_{\bar{x}}$
3	1.023	0.513	0.525	6.015	4.965
6	0.483	0.778	0.376	5.867	5.115
9	0.337	0.945	0.316	5.808	5.176

Mean values for this variable will fall between the control limits for a particular sample size by chance alone 99.73% of the time. For this reason it is generally unproductive to look for assignable causes when variation is confined within these limits. On the other hand, if the results fall outside the limits, the probability is high that an assignable cause was involved, and prompt action should be taken to try to identify the source of the problem.

6-3.1   Control Limits and Arithmetical Rounding Off

In Chapter 2, reference was made to the fact that in quality-control work it is sometimes permissible to report calculations to one more decimal place than is found in the actual measurements. It is here that this rule is applied. The mean of the means and the control limits have been reported to the third decimal place in each of the preceding examples, and the purpose of this is to remove any ambiguity about the location of any particular $\bar{x}$ value. For example, the value of 6.01 for sample 1 in Table 6-1 falls below the $\text{UCL}_{\bar{x}}$ of 6.015 and is therefore not considered to be statistically out of control. Similarly, a value of 4.97 would be clearly seen to be just inside the $\text{LCL}_{\bar{x}}$ for this variable and sample size. Had the limits been to the second decimal place, there would have been some doubt whether to consider 6.01 and 4.97 as being on, above, or below the limits.

6–3.2   Control Limits and Process Capability

We have said that $A_2\bar{R}$ is the equivalent of $3\sigma_{\bar{x}}$, so we can calculate $\sigma_{\bar{x}}$ from $A_2\bar{R}$ and hence make an estimate of the population standard deviation. For example, for samples of size 3,

$$A_2\bar{R} = 0.525$$

$$3\sigma_{\bar{x}} = 0.525$$

$$\sigma_{\bar{x}} = 0.175$$

Hence $\sigma = \sigma_{\bar{x}} \sqrt{n}$
$$= 0.175 \sqrt{3}$$
$$= 0.303$$

Similarly, the estimates from the other sample sizes are as follows:

Sample Size	$A_2\bar{R}$	$\sigma_{\bar{x}}$	Estimate of σ
3	0.525	0.175	0.303
6	0.375	0.125	0.306
9	0.316	0.105	0.315

We might have guessed from the close correlation between $\bar{R}$ and sample size that $\bar{R}$ would be a better estimator of σ, and this is in fact the case. The maximum variation from the calculated value for σ (0.316) is only 4.1%, whereas by the method described in Chapter 5 it was 17.1%. We can therefore feel confident to use $\bar{R}$ in estimating the standard deviation of the population, and hence the process capability.

If our control data were collected in samples of six, we would proceed in the following manner:

$$\overline{R} = 0.778, \qquad A_2 = 0.483 \text{ (from table)}$$

$$A_2\overline{R} = 0.376$$

$$3\sigma_{\bar{x}} = 0.376$$

$$3\sigma = 3\sigma_{\bar{x}}\sqrt{n}$$

$$= 0.376\sqrt{6}$$

$$= 0.921$$

$$= 0.92$$

That is,

$$\text{Process capability} = 5.49 \pm 0.92$$

$$= 4.57 \text{ to } 6.41$$

Note that the minimum and maximum values in process capability are **not** control limits; **they are the extremes of actual measurements** which we expect to find and consequently must be rounded off to the same number of decimal places as found in the measured values.

6-4   CALCULATION OF CONTROL LIMITS FOR RANGE

We have seen that the mean values can be expected to occur over a specific range depending on the sample size, that $\overline{R}$ is used as an estimator of this range, and that 99.73% of the means will fall between $\bar{x} \pm 3\sigma_{\bar{x}}$ **in the long run.**

A similar situation exists for range, except that we have the problem that range values are not normally distributed. In fact, the distribution of the ranges is slightly skewed (i.e., unevenly distributed about the mean), and there is less scope for variation below the mean than there is for variation above the mean. The theory associated with this distribution is beyond the scope of the present text, but the interested reader might refer to *Quality Control and Industrial Statistics* by Acheson J. Duncan (Richard D. Irwin, Inc., Homewood, Illinois). Instead, we will simply look at the application of the theory and the use of the constants which with A_2 are contained in Appendix 5. The constant for the lower control limit is D_3 and that for the upper control limit is D_4. The appropriate formulas are as follows:

$$LCL_R = D_3\overline{R}$$

$$UCL_R = D_4\overline{R}$$

where UCL_R = upper control limit for range
          LCL_R = lower control limit for range

Our variable example would give the following tabulation of values.

Sample Size	$\overline{R}$	D_3	LCL_R	D_4	UCL_R
3	0.513	0	0	2.575	1.321
6	0.778	0	0	2.004	1.559
9	0.945	0.184	0.174	1.816	1.716

As with the limits for mean, we consider any value for R which falls outside these limits to be statistically out of control.

6-5   OUT OF CONTROL

We must draw attention at this point to the difference between being **technically** out of control and being **statistically** out of control. The former term is generally used to indicate that a process has deteriorated and that some technically undesirable condition exists. This could mean that a maximum specification limit is being exceeded, that a minimum specification limit is not being reached, or that the process is varying to such an extent that the UCL_R is being exceeded.

The term "statistically out of control" on the other hand can refer to both technical deterioration and to technical improvement. Results which are **significantly below a maximum** specification limit, **significantly above a minimum** specification limit, or where the process is varying to such a slight extent that R values fall at or below the LCL_R are all cases where the process may be technically very much in control, but nevertheless statistically out of control.

We consider that a statistically out of control condition exists when either $\overline{x}$ or R values fall outside their respective limits, whether the extreme value indicates an improvement or a deterioration in the process from a technical point of view. The important principle involved is that it does not matter in which direction a change has taken place; if a value falls outside any control limit, there is a high probability that it is associated with an assignable cause which can be tracked down and identified. **We are therefore able to make improvements to processes by identifying assignable causes of improvements, as well as assignable causes of deterioration.**

6-6   DRAWING UP THE TABLES

Having decided to collect samples or subgroups of results of variables in a particular plant and to keep track of the means and ranges of these subgroups, the next step is to design a suitable standard form for the collection of these data. The decision about sample size will be discussed more fully in Chapter 7, but in the meantime it is appropriate to note that, if a number of variables are being included in the quality-control program, they may not all be collected in the same size of sample. Rather than draw up separate forms for each sample size, it is preferable to draw up one form with enough columns to accommodate the largest. This one form will then do for all variables. A typical example of a suitable form might be as shown in Figure 6-2(a). This form has the following features:

1. Provision for the name or description of the variable.
2. Provision for recording the production center so that the variability of different centers can be recorded (see Section 5-3 on homogeneity of samples).
3. Provision for recording the period of time from the first to the last sample on that particular sheet.
4. A reminder of the sample size to be used in case the sheets have the variable and the production center typed in before distribution to the quality-control technician.
5. A column headed with either Sample or Subgroup Number, depending on preference. In process industries where the analyses of a number of."samples" of material are being collected, the term "subgroup" may be preferred to avoid confusion between two connotations of the word "sample."
6. Use the bottom line to collect the sums of the means and ranges.
7. A column to record the sum of the x values prior to dividing by the sample size.

X̄ – R Records

Variable: _____   Period: From _____ To _____

Producton Center: _____   Sample Size: _____

Sample (or Subgroup) Number	Individual Values (x)										Σx	$\bar{x}$	R
	1	2	3	4	5	6	7	8	9	10			
											Σ		

(a)

Figure 6–2 Typical X̄-R Record Sheets

With the widespread use of electronic calculators, it might be felt that the $\sum x$ column is superfluous. It certainly has a function when the addition is being done manually, but when a calculator is being used, the total is immediately divided by the sample size, eliminating the need to record the total. In fact, with some calculators preprogrammed for mean and standard deviation, the Xn key is pressed after each x value (instead of +) and the $\bar{x}$ key after all the subgroup values are in. This gives a direct value for the mean without out the total even being displayed.

The space saved from the elimination of the $\sum x$ column could be used to add one or two additional x columns or to provide more room in each x column. Alternatively, it could provide space to re-

$\overline{X}$ - R Records

Variable: _____   Period: From _____ To _____

Production Center: _____   Subgroup Size: _____

Period		Individual Values (x)										$\overline{x}$	R
From	To	1	2	3	4	5	6	7	8	9	10		
												Σ	

(b)

Figure 6–2   (cont.)

cord a time period for each sample in place of a consecutive sample number. Figure 6-2(b) illustrates this modification.

In mass-production industries, samples of a given size are drawn simultaneously from a batch, measured, recorded, and another sample drawn. Under these conditions, consecutive sample numbers are most appropriate to use, as many will be taken in one day. Where individual measurements are made over a period of hours or even days, $\overline{x} - R$ charts can still provide useful controls, but it is probably more appropriate to record the time period over which each subgroup of values was collected rather than to use consecutive sample numbers.

6-7   USEFULNESS OF CHARTS

A question that is often asked is, why bother with charts at all? If we have all the data collected in a systematic manner in the record sheets, why not just pin these sheets to a tack board in the quality-control department and let anyone who is interested look at them to check to see if everything is under control? The answer is that a chart is a visual presentation of data which enables a large amount of information to be condensed into a minimum amount of space and still give the observer an impression of the variations in a process over a fairly long period of time. One of the features which a chart will show which cannot be seen simply by looking at the current record sheets is a gradual change in a process mean.

6-8   SHIFT IN THE PROCESS MEAN

Figure 6-3 is an example of shift in the process mean. Had only record sheets been used, the observer would note that in each month some values were above and some below the aimed·at mean and that none of the values fell outside the control limits. That person would then most likely assume that everything was within control. An observation of the chart, however, shows that, although the values fluctuate in a random manner, there is an apparent decline in the process mean from January to the middle of March. In fact, the mean for January is 3.35%, for February it is 3.27%, and for the first half of March it is 3.25%. Such a gradual shift in the process mean is unlikely to be spotted simply by observing the table of values, but our eye quickly catches the change as we scan the chart. We would have been prompted to examine the process long before the middle of March had the chart been in use.

Whether the number of samples being taken is large or small, this is one of the strongest arguments in favor of the use of charts. A gradual change in the process mean can be seen and **stopped** before the quality characteristic falls outside of specification. Not only that, but if we find from past records that the **mean** has tended to oscillate from a high to a low and then back up to a high, the control limits have probably been established for this condition. Once this oscillating has been identified and stopped, new control limits should be established. These new limits will cover a narrower range and will therefore give an earlier indication of an out-of-

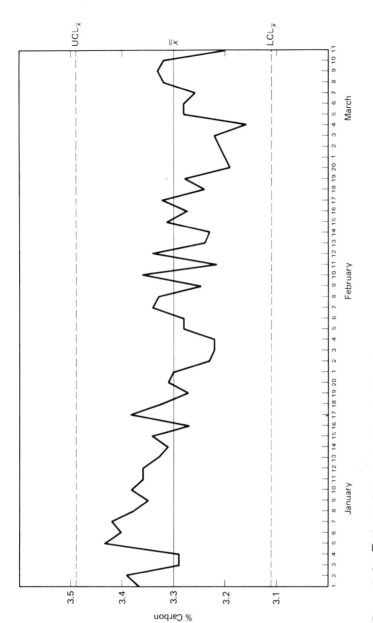

Figure 6–3 $\bar{x}$ Chart of Percent Carbon in Cast Iron

113

control condition should the process mean start to change at some future date.

6-9   CHART APPEARANCE

A chart is a visual presentation of data, and if it is to be used over a long period of time, it must be easy to look at and the key information should stand out clearly and unambiguously. In other words, it must have eye appeal. To accomplish this we must pay attention to a number of factors which influence the appearance of the charts. They do nothing for the facts in the case, but they tend to ensure that they will continue to be examined by the appropriate personnel. After all, quality-control programs have sometimes gone into disuse simply because people just stopped looking at the charts.

Some of these factors are as follows:

1. It is not necessary to be a draftsman or an artist to print legibly, but the tidier it is, the better. If there is more than one person available to do the lettering, have it done by the person whose work is most pleasing to the eye.

2. A chart should be large enough to show a portion of the past data from which the limits were calculated and have enough space for future entries so that any **trends** or **cyclical changes** can be observed as they take place. A trend is a long-run tendency for a change in the mean. It may consist of a decline, as shown in Figure 6-3, or it may be the opposite, a long-run increase. On the other hand, it may consist of a shift to the majority of the values being above the mean or a shift to their being mainly below the mean.

The actual size of the paper used depends to some extent on the number of charts to be drawn. Regular 8½ in. by 11 in. sheets of graph paper will serve the purpose in a great many cases, and they have the advantage of being readily filed away after they have been completed. Where large numbers of samples are concerned, however, we would be constantly drawing up new charts if we used the 8½ in. by 11 in. size, so 16 in. by 20 in. (or larger) would be more appropriate.

3. A quality-control chart is not an engineering drawing. While the points must be plotted accurately, the lines joining them should not be so fine and narrow that you can scarcely see them unless you are standing close up. In fact, it is preferable if you can see the lines

from 20 feet away. So do not be afraid to use a felt pen, but be sure to use black or some color which contrasts with the color of the graph paper. If, because of the width of the felt-pen lines, it is not clear whether a point is below or over a control limit line, remember that when it gets as close as this it is worth taking the time to check the $\bar{x}-R$ record sheet. In any case, **any point which exceeds control limits should be clearly circled so that there is no doubt in anyone's mind that an out-of-control condition exists.**

4. The key information on the charts should be clearly visible, so if a felt pen is used to join up the $\bar{x}$ and R values, the same or similar should be used for $\bar{\bar{x}}$, $\bar{R}$, and control limit lines, as these must also be clearly visible. It is necessary, however, to differentiate between means and control-limit lines, and the simplest method of doing this is to use a solid line for $\bar{\bar{x}}$ and $\bar{R}$ and a broken, or dotted, line for all control limits (or vice versa). The differentiation between the lines will also be enhanced if a color code is used. For example, black for the variable lines, green for $\bar{\bar{x}}$ and $\bar{R}$, and red for all control limits.

5. There must be a clear separation between the two charts, and they should be one above the other. This visual separation is accomplished by lining-in in black the scaled portions of the vertical axis which pertain to each chart; and this should be done at both ends. This increases the ease with which the observer differentiates between the two charts and reduces the risk of reading values in one chart and interpolating them up or down into the other. If the scale on the vertical axis is one continuous line, the risk of this is increased.

In any case, **there must always be a space between UCL$_R$ and LCL$_{\bar{x}}$ so that there is some place for out-of-control values to be plotted.** If the two charts are jammed close together, then an OOC (out-of-control) $\bar{x}$ value on the low side will run into the R chart and an OOC R value on the high side will run into the $\bar{x}$ chart. The resulting intertwining of lines can be extremely confusing.

Charts prepared in this manner not only have a more dramatic appearance, they are also easier to read. It is not necessary to peer over them at close range to obtain the information you are looking for; you may be able to see it from the other side of the room.

Figures 6-4 and 6-5 have been prepared from the data already established from our example on the effects of sample size, and they illustrate the various factors mentioned in this section.

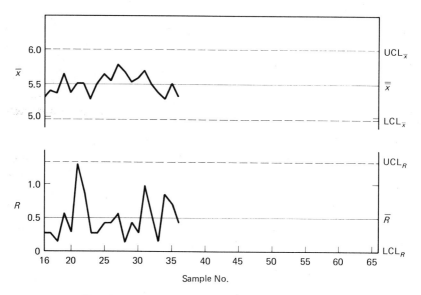

Figure 6–4   x̄-R Chart for Variable Example in Subgroups of 3

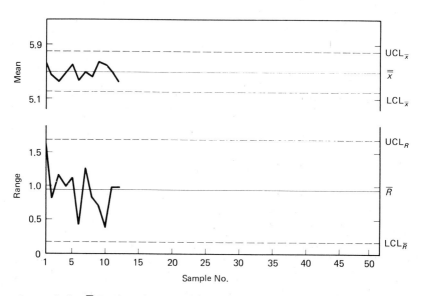

Figure 6–5   x̄-R Chart for Variable Example in Sub-Grups of 9

6-10   CHART SCALE

Deciding on the scale to use poses one of the greatest problems to many students, so we must establish some rules with regards to this. First, the subdivisions of the graph paper must not be made to represent a degree of accuracy greater than that of the actual measurements. For example, in the case of our example to illustrate the effects of sample size, the measurements were made to the second decimal place. Any subdivision on the graph paper must therefore not be made to represent any less than 0.01. It may represent more, but not less. The purpose of this is to avoid the "disease" which has already been mentioned, that of "delusions of accuracy." Some very practical-minded people will be looking at these charts, and they will become very cynical about them if they purport to show an accuracy greater than is actually achieved in the shop.

The second requirement is that the scale must be such as to allow both the $\overline{x}$ and the R charts to appear on the same sheet. This is not much of a problem when the larger sheets of graph paper are used, but it can be when using the $8\frac{1}{2}$ in. by 11 in. size. The purpose here is to allow the eye to scan both measures of variability ($\overline{x}$ and R) simultaneously and thus enable those who are constantly using the charts to build up a mental image of each specific quality characteristic.

The third requirement is that both the $\overline{x}$ and the R charts must be to the same scale. If we do not do this, then one or other will give a **visual** impression of less variation than actually exists. When we scan the charts, a vertical distance on one should have the same numerical value as on the other. Otherwise, our mental image of the variable will tend to be inaccurate.

Using Figure 6-4 as an example, the procedure used was as follows:

1. Decide in which direction the paper will lie. In this case, with an $8\frac{1}{2}$ in. by 11 in. sheet, the page must lie horizontally to allow sufficient space for future values.

2. Count the subdivisions on the vertical axis. There are 7×10 or 70 subdivisions with this paper. Then deduct an inch for space between the two charts, thus leaving 60 subdivisions.

3. Count the minimum numerical "distance" required for the two charts:

$$\text{LCL}_{\bar{x}} \text{ to UCL}_{\bar{x}} = 4.97 \text{ to } 6.02 = 1.05$$

$$\text{LCL}_R \text{ to UCL}_R = \quad 0 \text{ to } 1.32 = 1.32$$

$$\text{Total} \quad 2.37$$

4. Now divide 2.37 by the available space (60) and we get 0.04. This is an awkward value to use as it means that **two and a half subdivisions would represent 0.1.** This would create difficulties in plotting the points on the chart, so we round the 0.04 up to 0.05. **Two subdivisions will now represent 0.1.**

5. Mark off the scaled portion at the bottom for the R chart, starting at 0, and then position the $\bar{x}$ chart scale so as to allow room at the top for the eventuality of an OOC point above $\text{UCL}_{\bar{x}}$. It is not possible to have a range value less than zero, so there is no need for any space to be left below LCL_R. A similar procedure was used for Figure 6-5, except that in this case space had to be left below LCL_R as we have a LCL_R greater than zero because of the sample size.

6-11   NAMING THE CHARTS

It is absolutely imperative that each chart should have a title naming the quality characteristic being measured, the production center, if appropriate, and the sample size. Decisions are sometimes made to change sample size depending on whether there has been an increase or a decrease in the amount of testing, and, as control limits are dependent in part on sample size, this should appear on all charts.

In addition, the units of measurement must also be stated. It is possible for a quality characteristic to be measured in different ways and in different units, so these should always be stated to avoid confusion.

It was not by accident that neither the name of the variable nor its units were given in Figures 5-2 through 5-4 and Figures 6-4 and 6-5. These were presented in order to illustrate and emphasize the effects of sample size, and the reader was free to imagine the values as inches of length, millimeters of diameter, percentage of zinc, or any other quality characteristic whatsoever that might seem to be appropriate. Additional information might only have confused the issue. This practice is accept-

able in a textbook where one particular factor is being emphasized; it is not acceptable in plant quality-control charts.

QUESTIONS AND PROBLEMS

---

1. Why is it necessary to use samples of equal size when calculating the mean of the means from the formula $\bar{\bar{x}} = (\sum \bar{x})/n$?

2. (a) What are chance causes of variation?
   (b) What are the sources of chance causes of variation?
   (c) Why can chance variations never be entirely eliminated from a process?
   (d) Describe fully what is meant by "assignable causes of variation."

3. Give an example, from each of the areas which would be examined, of a typical question which might be asked when attempting to identify the source of an assignable cause of variation.

4. What happens to the variation between the sample means and the average range within the samples as sample size increases?

5. At what level do we set the upper and lower control limits for sample means?

6. Show, in step form and by the use of the correct symbols, how process capability can be estimated from the control limits for means.

7. (a) Describe what is meant by a process being technically out of control.
   (b) Describe what is meant by a process being statistically out of control.
   (c) Why is it advantageous to identify all results which are statistically out of control, even if they are technically within control?

8. Without reference to any textbook or notes, design a form for the collection of $\bar{x} - R$ data. Be sure to include space for recording all information which might be of value in identifying this particular collection of data. Where a choice of format has to be made, explain the reason for your choice.

9. Describe a reason why charts are an essential component of an effective control program and why $\bar{x}-R$ record sheets, by themselves, are insufficient.

10. Describe three of the factors which must be taken into account when considering the visual appeal of $\bar{x}-R$ charts.

11. Describe two requirements which must be kept in mind when deciding on the scale to use for an $\bar{x}-R$ chart.

7

Starting Up the Control System for Variables

7-1 *DECIDING ON WHICH VARIABLES TO CHART*

Having decided that a quality-control program would be advantageous, the next questions to ask are "Which variables should be charted, and should there be a breakdown by production center?" Unfortunately, there are no simple answers to these questions as so much depends on the existing testing and inspection procedures and on whether or not a full-time person will be hired to take over the quality-control function. In a large company, where records are already being kept on a large number of standard products, there is no doubt that the organizing and analysis of past records would require a full-time commitment right from the start if reasonable progress is to be made.

The small- to medium-sized company, on the other hand, may never have the budget to cover a full-time quality-control specialist, and the duties may have to be carried by one or more persons in addition to their existing responsibilities. It is here, therefore, that the decision as to which variables to chart is most critical. If you undertake to chart too many variables, then the extra time involved may become a burden and you may drop the whole idea. It is better to start small and let the function grow as you become accustomed to its demands on your time. Remember that quality-control work cannot be put off. The calculation and plotting of $\bar{x}$ and R points takes very little time indeed, but it is the fact that they have to be done immediately the information becomes available that creates the problem. Quality-control information is of limited use if it arrives a week late and is of maximum use when it can identify and stop an out-of-control condition as soon as it occurs. The task of recording the information must therefore be given to someone who is prepared to, and is able to, stop whatever he or she is doing and process the quality-control data as soon as it is generated.

It is a good idea to use the principle of management by exception under these circumstances and to start off by charting only those variables which are known in advance to be a source of problems. In this way, you will obtain the greatest benefits from your efforts. The problem here is that you may not know the true sources of your problems until after the first analysis of your records, as your current opinion may be based on biased observations. This initial analysis is so important that it is the subject of a separate section in this chapter.

Another factor involved in the decision about what to chart is whether or not the end product has to meet a recognized specification or standard. If the product is a part which is machined to a dimensional specification and there has been trouble meeting that specification, then there should be no doubt about one decision. An $\bar{x}-R$ chart should be set up for that particular part. Similarly, if the product has to meet some minimum specification for a property, such as strength or hardness, then you should set up charts to keep this property under close scrutiny and also to know what the probability would be of falling outside the specification.

In the case of a property, however, we may be faced with an additional decision. The properties of the product are determined by other factors, and these factors may also have to be the subjects of control charts. Properties may be affected by temperature, pressure, humidity, or other physical conditions during the processing, or by some chemical constituent in the product itself, and one or more of these may be of particular significance. Known technology may dictate precisely which factors are significant, and in the initial stages these alone should be charted, as well as the property, in order not to be distracted from the prime task of improving the product's ability to meet specification.

Where the technology does not exist or is not known, and where other statistical techniques are not available, there may be no alternative other than to chart all the available information until such time as a relationship between a factor, or factors, and the specified property becomes apparent.

When the product is being manufactured at more than one production center and is not being segregated by center for inspection purposes, leave things as they are and do not make changes at this stage. Only if the study of the variable indicates the possibility of there being more than one universe of values should the extra time and effort be devoted to the segregation and evaluation of the individual production centers. Only then is the extra work likely to pay off in closer control.

7-2   HISTORICAL DATA

If existing testing or inspection measurements have been recorded in the past, then this information can be used to obtain reasonably reliable provisional values for process means and for control limits. There are a few precautions which have to be observed, however.

First, it must be remembered that historical records are frequently kept by the department or personnel doing the actual measuring, and people are less prone to question their own work than that of someone else. In other words, whereas the quality-control-oriented person is likely to question any unusual results, and has a "yardstick" against which to make comparisons, the inspector or chemist is likely to accept all results, no matter how unlikely, provided they fall within the specification or guidelines to which he or she is working. Values which are statistically out of control, but which may be either technically under control or out of control, may therefore be found in past records.

In addition, people have been known to play the occasional joke to relieve the boredom of a monotonous job, and it has been known for a ridiculous figure to be put among others in a report to "test" to see if "the boss" really reads these reports that are sent to him. This could be good for a few laughs for a couple of days, especially if there is no comeback, but unfortunately the spurious value then becomes part of the permanent record. Fortunately, if the initial analysis is properly conducted, these far-out values will be identified and eliminated before control limits are established.

7-3   ANALYZING HISTORICAL DATA: CONTROL LIMITS

It is generally accepted that control limits should not be based on any less than 25 subgroups, so it is necessary to go far enough into the past to ensure obtaining more than this number. The values should then be taken from the records in consecutive order and collected into subgroups of a suitable size.

The $\bar{x}$ and R values are found for each subgroup, and hence $\bar{\bar{x}}$, $\bar{R}$ and the control limits. The $\bar{x}$ column is then scanned to ascertain if any values are below $\text{LCL}_{\bar{x}}$ and then scanned again to see if any are above $\text{UCL}_{\bar{x}}$. If any are found to be outside the limits they are either circled or marked OOC in red. This procedure is then repeated for the R values.

The results are collected in samples or subgroups because the central limit theorem tells us that the means will be normally distributed, and we will be able to make statistical inferences from the results obtained. Any out-of-control subgroups must therefore be removed from our calculations in order that our limits will be based only on those results which are likely to be normally distributed. It is important to remember that it is the subgroup which is out of control if **either** $\bar{x}$ or R is beyond the limits. To remove **all** effects of an out-of-control subgroup, it is therefore necessary to remove both its $\bar{x}$ and R values from the calculations.

Table 7-1 is typical of a table of results from past records, and the steps involved were as follows:

1. $\bar{x}$ and R were calculated for each subgroup.
2. $\bar{x}$ and R columns were summed to give

$$\Sigma \bar{x} = 105.49; \qquad \Sigma R = 9.26$$

3. $\bar{\bar{x}}$ and $\bar{R}$ were computed as

$$\bar{\bar{x}} = \frac{105.49}{28}$$

$$= 3.768\%$$

$$\bar{R} = \frac{9.26}{28}$$

$$= 0.331\%$$

Table 7-1 $\bar{x} - R$ RECORDS

$\bar{x} - R$ Records

Variable: % Carbon Equivalent in Class 50 Cast Iron

Production Center: Cupola No. 1

Subgroup Size: 6

Sub Group No.	% Carbon Equivalent (x) 1	2	3	4	5	6	Σx	$\bar{x}$	R	
1	3.66	3.75	3.95	3.58	3.59	3.61	22.14	3.690	0.37	
2	3.95	3.99	4.12	3.95	3.75	4.12	23.88	(3.980)	0.37	00C
3	3.87	3.75	3.89	3.64	3.60	3.71	22.46	3.743	0.29	
4	3.64	3.68	3.46	3.64	3.75	3.59	21.76	3.627	0.29	
5	4.07	3.76	3.39	3.60	3.60	3.59	22.01	3.668	(0.68)	00C
6	3.68	3.79	3.71	3.64	3.63	3.92	22.37	3.728	0.29	
7	3.83	3.79	3.74	3.67	3.68	3.64	22.35	3.725	0.19	
8	3.84	3.76	3.80	3.78	3.75	3.78	22.71	3.785	0.09	
9	3.85	3.86	3.62	3.61	3.61	3.77	22.32	3.720	0.25	
10	3.71	3.87	3.77	3.69	3.59	3.54	22.17	3.695	0.33	
11	3.67	3.74	3.84	3.78	3.89	3.76	22.68	3.780	0.22	
12	3.77	3.62	3.73	3.58	3.84	3.86	22.40	3.733	0.28	
13	3.76	3.80	3.61	3.80	4.08	3.72	22.77	3.795	0.47	
14	3.59	3.61	3.62	3.65	3.82	3.92	22.21	3.702	0.33	
15	3.76	3.97	3.65	3.98	4.02	3.75	23.13	3.855	0.37	
16	3.67	3.82	3.70	3.74	3.76	3.75	22.44	3.740	0.15	
17	3.78	3.97	4.06	3.97	3.63	3.80	23.21	3.868	0.43	
18	3.94	3.78	3.44	3.91	3.49	3.49	22.05	3.675	0.50	
19	3.63	3.91	3.60	3.50	3.61	4.03	22.28	3.713	0.53	
20	3.78	3.70	3.83	3.75	3.85	4.12	23.03	3.838	0.42	
21	3.91	4.08	3.81	3.86	3.91	4.01	23.58	(3.930)	0.27	00C
22	3.77	3.84	3.61	3.82	3.84	3.94	22.82	3.803	0.33	
23	3.80	3.76	3.69	3.60	3.96	3.71	22.52	3.753	0.36	
24	3.71	3.73	3.83	3.75	4.02	3.74	22.78	3.797	0.31	
25	3.82	3.81	3.57	3.87	3.76	4.00	22.83	3.805	0.43	
26	3.77	3.89	3.73	3.82	3.72	3.73	22.66	3.777	0.17	
27	3.95	3.99	3.92	3.78	3.80	3.57	23.01	3.835	0.42	
28	3.68	3.80	3.70	3.72	3.70	3.77	22.37	3.728	0.12	
							Σ	105.49	9.26	

4. Control limits were then found:

$$\text{UCL}_{\bar{x}} = 3.768 + (0.483 \times 0.331)$$

$$= 3.768 + 0.160$$

$$= 3.928\%$$

$$\text{LCL}_{\bar{x}} = 3.768 - (0.483 \times 0.331)$$

$$= 3.768 - 0.160$$

$$= 3.608\%$$

$$\text{UCL}_R = 2.004 \times 0.331$$
$$= 0.663\%$$
$$\text{LCL}_R = 0$$

5. The $\bar{x}$ column was then scanned, and it was found that subgroups 2 and 21 were out of control above $\text{UCL}_{\bar{x}}$. These were then circled to draw attention to the fact that they would have to be removed. The R column was then scanned, and it was found that subgroup 5 was out of control above UCL_R. This value was also circled.

6. The $\bar{x}$ and R values for each of the out-of-control subgroups were then subtracted from $\sum \bar{x}$ and $\sum R$ respectively.

$$\text{Revised } \sum \bar{x} = 105.49 - (3.980 + 3.668 + 3.930)$$

$$= 93.91$$

$$\text{Revised } \sum R = 9.26 - (0.37 + 0.68 + 0.27)$$

$$= 7.94$$

7. Revised values for $\bar{\bar{x}}$ and $\bar{R}$ were then computed as

$$\text{Revised } \bar{\bar{x}} = \frac{93.91}{25}$$

$$= 3.756\%$$

$$\text{Revised } \bar{R} = \frac{7.94}{25}$$

$$= 0.318\%$$

8. Revised control limits were then established as

$$\text{UCL}_{\bar{x}} = 3.756 + (0.483 \times 0.318)$$

$$= 3.756 + 0.154$$

$$= 3.910\%$$

$$\text{LCL}_{\bar{x}} = 3.756 - 0.154$$

$$= 3.602\%$$

$$\text{UCL}_R = 2.004 \times 0.318$$

$$= 0.637\%$$

$$\text{LCL}_R = 0$$

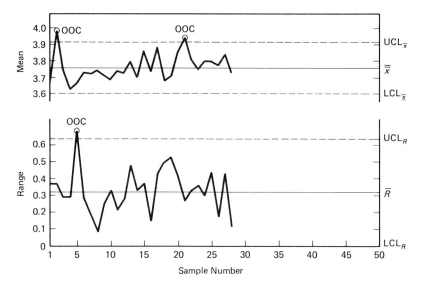

Figure 7-1 $\bar{x}$-R Chart for Percent Carbon Equivalent in Class 50 Cast Iron

9. The $\bar{x}$ and R columns were then scanned again and it was found that no new points were out of control.
   Note: This second check of the columns must not be omitted as it is sometimes found that the removal of some seriously out-of-control points then leaves other points out of control beyond the revised limits. The procedure sometimes has to be repeated two or three times before all out-of-control subgroups have been removed.

10. The control charts were then prepared, and these are shown in Figure 7-1. Note that the out-of-control values have been clearly identified. The chart must be an honest representation of what has actually happened and must show all results both good and bad. There must be no confusion here with the rationale for removing the OOC values from the calculations. This was done not to conceal, but in order to base our calculations only on results which were statistically within control.

7–4   ANALYZING HISTORICAL DATA: HISTOGRAMS

In Section 2-6.3, reference was made to the one big disadvantage of the electronic calculator; it does not provide a visual impression of the distribution of values. In the initial analysis of historical data such an impression may be helpful in determining whether or not the results should be lumped together or broken down by production center. As an example, take an industrial dispensing system with two units measuring out material to add to a process. Checks of the weight of material dispensed by both machines give the following results:

$$\text{Mean} = 2.75 \text{ kg}$$

$$\text{Standard deviation} = 0.27 \text{ kg}$$

$$\text{Coefficient of variation} = 9.8\%$$

$$\text{Process capability} = 2.8 \pm 0.8 \quad \text{or} \quad 2.0 \text{ to } 3.6 \text{ kg}$$

The coefficient of variation is on the high side, resulting in a wide process capability, and the distribution of results is then examined with the following results:

WEIGHT DISPENSED BY TWO UNITS (KG)

Weight	Frequency (%)
2.1	1
2.2	2
2.3	4
2.4	5
2.5	10
2.6	15
2.7	13
2.8	13
2.9	14
3.0	10
3.1	6
3.2	4
3.3	2
3.4	1
	100%

A look at the frequency column shows a drop in the middle where we expect to see a peak, and Figure 7-2 shows this graphically to better advantage.

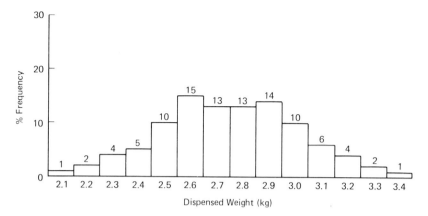

Figure 7–2 Histogram of Material Dispensed by Two Machines

Whenever we find a histogram which is flat along the top or shows evidence of having two modes (most frequently occurring value) we must suspect that we do not have a homogeneous sample. We must examine the possibility that more than one universe of values exists. In this case, we segregate the results for the two units and obtain the following:

Weight Dispensed (kg)	Frequency (%)	
	Unit 1	Unit 2
2.1	2	—
2.2	4	—
2.3	8	—
2.4	9	1
2.5	17	3
2.6	22	8
2.7	16	10
2.8	9	17
2.9	7	21
3.0	4	16
3.1	2	10
3.2	—	8
3.3	—	4
3.4	—	2
	100%	100%

	Unit 1	Unit 2
Mean ($\bar{x}$)	2.60 kg	2.91 kg
Standard deviation (s)	0.22 kg	0.21 kg
Coefficient of variation (v)	8.5%	7.2%
Process capability	2.6 ± 0.7 kg	2.9 ± 0.6 kg
	or	or
	1.9 to 3.3 kg	2.3 to 3.5 kg

Obviously, we have two different distributions here, one with a mean of 2.6 kg and the other with a mean of 2.9 kg. Figures 7-3 and 7-4 show these distributions to have reasonably uniform histograms, but occupying opposite ends of the total range of values. Each has a similar standard deviation, but they have been set up in such a way that their means are different, and when they come together the result is as shown in Figure 7-2. By making adjustments to one or other or both of the units, the means can be brought together, giving about a 20% reduction in the process capability range.

It should only be necessary to do this type of breakdown during the initial stages. After the two means have been made to coincide with one another, $\bar{x} - R$ charts can be set up to handle both sources of material. Should one of the means start to drift at a future date, this will show up as an increase in range or a change in the $\bar{\bar{x}}$ value.

This type of analysis should not be necessary with every quality characteristic included in the program, but it should be used where any abnormality in the distribution indicates the possibility of more than one universe being involved. However, it is important to remember that it is not necessary to have two or more machines to obtain the effect illustrated in this section. Where skill is a determining factor, two operators on different shifts can produce this effect from one machine.

7–5   STARTING FROM SCRATCH

In some small companies, record keeping is kept to a minimum, and the inspection and testing functions may simply be to identify off-specification product. There may be no records at all of the values for on-specification product. Or records may be kept of each test of a particular kind, but no identification made as to what was tested. That is, the routine checks and the extra tests conducted when prob-

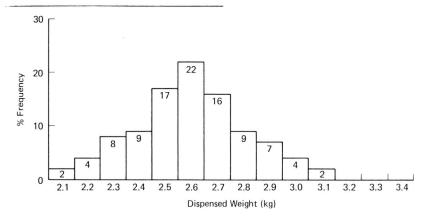

Figure 7-3 Histogram of Material Dispensed by Machine 1

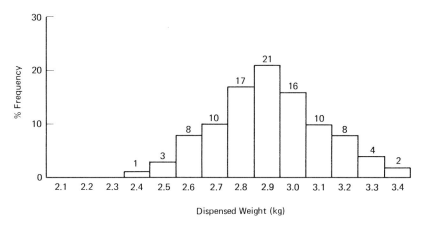

Figure 7-4 Histogram of Material Dispensed by Machine 2

lems existed were all mixed in together. Under either of these circumstances it is necessary to start from scratch and build up your own records.

It will be necessary first to introduce a recording system at the inspection or testing areas which ensures that every test is recorded and properly identified. The best approach is to design a form to suit your own particular needs and to have the testing personnel make their entries immediately after each test. Do not forget to discuss your proposed form with them prior to having them run off;

the person who has to fill it out may have some useful suggestions with regards to the allocation of space. Also, have the first batch run off by some inexpensive reproduction process, as it is the experience of a great many people that after a new form has been in use for about a month its shortcomings have been discovered and suggestions made for its modification.

Do not, at this stage, leave $\bar{x} - R$ record sheets with the testing people. You have still to decide on a suitable subgroup size, and you will not be able to do this until you have some idea of the rate at which the test results are generated. If you are going to involve others in the process, it is better to iron out all the problems first, do all the analyzing and chopping and changing, and only involve others when everything has stabilized and you know what direction you are going in.

As there are no past records from which to calculate control limits, you will not be able to draw up charts immediately, but this should be done as soon as is practically possible. One approach, in the initial stage, is to record the cumulative mean, as was done in Chapter 5, and when the results have stabilized within a narrow range, calculate control limits and set up your first provisional $\bar{x} - R$ charts. Remember that the purpose here is to make as early a start as possible to having a visual presentation of the data, and that you may not have enough information to accurately identify $\bar{\bar{x}}$, $\bar{R}$, and the control limits. As more results come in, you are likely to have to modify all the key information, so do not plan the charts too far into the future. It will depend on the stability of the process, but you may have to modify the limits a number of times before you are confident that they are truly representative of the process as it exists.

7-6   SAMPLE SIZE

We have seen that with a larger sample size we will tend to come close to the population mean sooner than with a small one and that the distribution of the means will more closely approach a normal distribution. These are positive arguments in favor of using as large a sample size as possible.

However, there is another factor to be considered, and that is **time.** For quality-control techniques to be most effective, the results should be available in as short a time as possible so that corrective action can be taken when necessary. If a large number of tests are made throughout the day, we should not have to wait until the end of the shift to find out if everything is under control. It is preferable to subdivide the results into smaller subgroups so that there can be feedback of information into the system at regular intervals of time. For example, if 40 tests are taken per day, the breakdown could be into four samples of ten, ten samples of four, five samples of eight, or eight samples of five results. In any case, the size and frequency of subgroups can be tailored to suit the needs of the individual system.

It must not be thought, however, that statistical quality-control techniques have to be confined to cases where large amounts of test data are being generated. It can have useful application even when only one value is generated per day. This may occur when a number of different grades of material are produced each day, and only one test, or series of tests, are taken from each. Charting can prevent confusion where any of the grade tests are similar and can keep a close watch on any tendency for the mean of the means to change over a period of time.

A sample size of four should be used under these circumstances, as this will ensure that at least one value will be plotted each week. Although most weeks have five days, some have only four because of a holiday on either a Friday or a Monday. Using a subgroup size of four will ensure that at least one and occasionally two results are plotted each week.

Another, although slightly more complex and time-consuming approach to the problem of deciding on sample size is to construct a graph similar to the one in Figure 6-1. Then, knowing the process capability for individual values in your study, you may decide that the sample size should be such as to encompass some given percentage of that range. For example, in the case used in Chapter 6, the process capability range in individual values was 1.90. If we wanted our samples to take a large enough bite of the population to ensure a mean range of 50% of this amount, $\bar{R}$ would be 0.95, and this would coincide with a sample size of nine. If you consider 40% to be satisfactory, this would mean an $\bar{R}$ value of 0.76 and a sample size of six. On the other hand, if the $\bar{R}$ value is to represent 30% of the process capability range, a sample size of four will suffice. The judgment here is strictly subjective and depends on what the person expects from a sampling system, but we must remember that the $\bar{R}$ value is only the expected value, and that by chance alone the range in a sample could reach the UCL_R level. Summarizing these three cases, we obtain the following **for our particular example from Chapter 6:**

Sample Size	$\bar{R}$ (from Formula)	$\bar{R}$ as % of PC Range	D_4	UCL_R	UCL_R as % of PC Range
9	0.94	49%	1.816	1.71	90%
6	0.77	41%	2.004	1.54	81%
4	0.60	32%	2.282	1.37	72%

In other words, if we took four random values from the 90 which were analyzed, we could expect that by chance alone their range could encompass 72% of the process capability range. This is a large proportion of the possible range for such a proportionately small sample, and this is one reason why even small samples produce successful control programs. Such a study requires the use of a statistical technique known as regression analysis, and this may be beyond the immediate scope of some readers of this book

7-7   AIMED-AT VALUE

When we are manufacturing something to a nominal size (or value) with a plus or minus tolerance, then $\bar{x}$ and nominal size should coincide with one another. If they do not, and the process capability conforms closely to the specification range (see Section 4-8), then by chance alone we can expect to find some of our product being off specification. That is, the process may be capable of meeting the specification, but fails to do so simply because of a shift in the mean. When an initial analysis of data shows that $\bar{\bar{x}}$ and nominal size do not coincide, then the charts should be set up so that control limits are based on nominal size and the equipment immediately adjusted so as to bring about the necessary change in $\bar{\bar{x}}$.

In the case of physical properties and residual chemical elements, however, such a simple solution may not be possible. There are often technical constraints on how high a property can go or how low an impurity can be taken. For example, if a process is producing some material with a tensile strength below the minimum specified, it is not satisfactory simply to raise the $LCL_{\bar{x}}$ and everything else by the amount that is necessary to meet the specification, because in the first place **control limits and specification limits are not the same**

thing. Control limits are always narrower than the process capability for the reasons explained when we examined the central limit theorem. Also, there are technical limitations on how high the maximum strength of any material can go, and simply moving everything up may make the $UCL_{\bar{x}}$ become unrealistic. Besides, if you are already close to the maximum possible for a material, the tightening up of the variables in the process is more likely to reduce the size of the range rather than to increase the mean. Simply moving everything upward, as can be done with a dimensional problem, may result in the acceptance of control limits which are wider than they should be and which may then mask results which are out of control. When an initial study indicates this type of condition, it would be preferable not to establish control limits immediately, but to start by tightening up the processes involved while at the same time recording only the new results. In other words, handle the establishment of control limits in the same way as you would if no historical records existed.

7-8   CONTROL LIMITS AND PROCESS CAPABILITY

In Sections 6-3.2 and 7-7, references were made to the differences between control limits and specification limits or process capability, and it may seem superfluous to pursue the matter further. However, this is an area which is so frequently misunderstood that an example will be given for illustrative purposes. Suppose that an examination of historical records gave the following results for a cast iron which was required to have a minimum tensile strength of 50,000 lb/in.^{2}.

$$\bar{\bar{x}} = 53,400 \text{ lb/in.}^2$$
$$\bar{R} = 4,100 \text{ lb/in.}^2$$

The results were collected in subgroups of four, so the control limits were found to be

$$A_2\bar{R} = 4,100 \times 0.729$$
$$= 2,990 \text{ lb/in.}^2$$
$$UCL_{\bar{x}} = 53,400 + 2,990 = 56,390 \text{ lb/in.}^2$$
$$LCL_{\bar{x}} = 53,400 - 2,990 = 50,010 \text{ lb/in.}^2$$

The lower control limit is slightly above the minimum technical specification, and the greatest mistake that can be made is to assume that this means that the process is within technical control.

The central limit theorem gave the relationship

$$\sigma = \sigma_{\bar{x}} \sqrt{n}$$

and we know that control limits are set at $3\sigma_{\bar{x}}$; therefore,

$$3\sigma = 3\sigma_{\bar{x}}\sqrt{n}$$
$$= A_2\bar{R}\,\sqrt{n}$$
$$= 2{,}990\,\sqrt{4}$$
$$= 5{,}980 \text{ lb/in.}^2$$

Therefore,

$$\text{Process capability} = 53{,}400 \pm 5{,}980 \text{ lb/in.}^2$$
$$= 47{,}470 \text{ to } 59{,}430 \text{ lb/in.}^2$$

So, by chance alone, we can expect some of our individual results to fall below the minimum of 50,000 lb/in.².

To find the probability of results falling below the minimum specified, we calculate the z value and hence the probability of being below 50,000 lb/in.²

$$z = \frac{53{,}400 - 50{,}000}{1{,}993}$$

$$= 1.71$$

$$\text{Area from } \bar{x} \text{ to } x = 0.456$$

$$\text{Area beyond } x = 0.044$$

That is, in the long run, 4.4% of the product can be expected to have a strength **below** the minimum requirement. This is the same as odds of 1 in 23 and, if one's life depended on it, one would not like to be taking this kind of chance.

So even if everything appears to be in order and there are no points which are **statistically** out of control, we must examine process capability to ensure that everything is within technical control.

7-9   CHANGE IN SAMPLE SIZE

Sometimes at the start of a quality-control program it is found that, after calculating everything for one size of sample, it appears to be more convenient to use another size. When this happens, it is not necessary to start all over again and rearrange all the values in different sized subgroups. The central limit theorem once again can come to our aid. Using the example from the previous section, for a subgroup size of four,

$$\bar{\bar{x}} = 53{,}400 \text{ lb/in.}^2$$

$$\bar{R} = \ \ 4{,}100 \text{ lb/in.}^2$$

$$\text{UCL}_{\bar{x}} = 56{,}390 \text{ lb/in.}^2$$

$$\text{LCL}_{\bar{x}} = 50{,}010 \text{ lb/in.}^2$$

Now if we want to change to a subgroup size of six, we first of all **estimate** standard deviation as we did before to find process capability.

$$3\sigma = 3\sigma_{\bar{x}}\sqrt{n}$$
$$= A_2\bar{R}\ \sqrt{n}$$
$$= 2{,}990\ \sqrt{4}$$
$$= 5{,}980 \text{ lb/in.}^2$$

We want to find the value of $A_2\bar{R}$ for a sample size of six, so we solve the equation for A_2R:

$$3\sigma = A_2\bar{R}\ \sqrt{n}$$

$$A_2\bar{R} = \frac{3\sigma}{\sqrt{n}}$$

$$= \frac{5{,}980}{\sqrt{6}}$$

$$= 2{,}440 \text{ lb/in.}^2$$

From this we can also find the expected value for $\overline{R}$ by looking in the tables for the A_2 value which corresponds to the sample size of six. Hence

$$\overline{R} = \frac{2{,}440}{A_2}$$

$$= \frac{2{,}440}{0.483}$$

$$= 5{,}050 \text{ lb/in.}^2$$

The control chart information for a subgroup size of six is therefore

$$\overline{\overline{x}} = 53{,}400 \text{ lb/in.}^2$$

$$\overline{R} = 5{,}050 \text{ lb/in.}^2$$

$$\text{UCL}_{\overline{x}} = 53{,}400 + 2{,}440 = 55{,}840 \text{ lb/in.}^2$$

$$\text{LCL}_{\overline{x}} = 53{,}400 - 2{,}440 = 50{,}960 \text{ lb in.}^2$$

New limits can now be set up and a quick change made to the new subgroup size.

7-10   LOCATION OF CHARTS

In Section 7-5, reference was made to the possibility of leaving $\bar{x}-R$ record sheets with inspection personnel and that this should not be done until everything had stabilized. This, of course, may raise the question, why do that at all? Why not have someone concentrate all their efforts on quality control and gain the benefits of specialization? This person, or persons, will become more and more competent in the statistical analysis of the data generated. To the person doing the testing, the $\bar{x}-R$ records may be just an additional chore. That is the negative view of course. The big advantage to the subdivision of responsibilities is the advantage of speed. When the person doing the testing also enters the values in an $\bar{x}-R$ report and computes the mean and the range, we have the fastest possible way of finding out if a subgroup is out of control.

One approach is to paint lines on a blackboard to make it similar to an $\bar{x}-R$ record sheet and position it at the testing or inspection station. This board must have the control limits clearly shown above the table so that the person entering the results can clearly see if an out-of-control condition has occurred and can notify the appropriate person immediately. No charts are necessary at this point.

Such a system will permit getting the best of both worlds. The board entries will ensure an early warning of problems, and the information will then be recorded in a permanent manner at the end of each day or shift. The person making the permanent entries in tables and charts can be the person with overall quality-control responsibilities, who will look out for long-term changes in the population mean and conduct other statistical analyses.

There are many ways in which the quality-control function can be organized, but two of the most important considerations to be taken into account must always be speed of reporting and permanence of records.

7-11   SUMMARIZING RESULTS

Like any other staff department, quality-control personnel must keep higher management informed of their activities and of the effects of these activities. One method of doing this is to prepare a summary report form which is submitted on each plotted characteristic at suitable intervals. It is all very fine to have a room in which charts are displayed for the benefit of all concerned with process control, but for the busy general manager who wants to know what has happened and what was done about it, nothing can quite compare with a summary report.

Summary reports should be prepared at regular intervals, either once a month or after every 20 or 30 additional samples and should contain the following information:

Name of variable

Name or number of production center

Period of time covered

Aimed-at mean value

Current $\bar{\bar{x}}$, $\bar{R}$, and control limits

Previous $\bar{\bar{x}}$, $\bar{R}$, and control limits

Cumulative $\bar{\bar{x}}$, $\bar{R}$, and control limits

Date or time of any out-of-control values

Cause of any out-of-control values

Action taken to prevent a recurrence of this type of out-of-control condition

Action taken to correct a change in the $\bar{\bar{x}}$ value

Comments

Some conditions may necessitate the inclusion of additional technical information for identification purposes, but the statistical information will be of considerable use to the busy manager and will help him or her to keep in touch with what is happening in the area of quality control.

QUESTIONS AND PROBLEMS

1. If a property of a product is to be the subject of an $\bar{x}-R$ chart, what might also have to be charted concurrently?

2. List, in chronological order, the steps which must be taken when using historical data to calculate provisional control limits for new $\bar{x}-R$ charts.

3. (a) What kind of evidence would induce you to break down results by production centers in order to determine whether or not a homogeneous population exists?
   (b) What method would you use to determine whether or not a population is homogeneous?

4. When starting from scratch with no historical data, what procedure might be used to determine the earliest possible opportunity for the calculation of provisional control limits?

5. (a) State an argument in favor of the use of large samples or subgroups.
   (b) State an argument in favor of the use of relatively small samples or subgroups.

6. The mean of a high-impact-resisting material is below the aimed-at value, producing an unacceptable probability that some results may fall below the minimum specification. What action should be taken
   (a) With regard to the process of manufacture or treatment?
   (b) With regard to the charting of results?

7. The $\text{UCL}_{\bar{x}}$ for a variable being greater than its maximum specification value does not guarantee that the maximum specification will not be exceeded. Explain why this statement is correct.

8. Show, in step form and by the use of the correct symbols, how to estimate control limits for one size of subgroups from information obtained for another size of subgroup.

9. Design a board for the collection of $\bar{x}-R$ information at an inspection station.

10. Take the tensile strength values from Table 2-4 and arrange them in subgroups of three. Start at the top of the first column and go down each column in succession. Calculate $\bar{x}$ and R for each subgroup and control limits, and draw up $\bar{x}-R$ charts. Repeat the process using subgroups of six and comment on any differences which are found.

11. The following are values for percentage of chromium in an alloy iron. The results have been tabulated consecutively from column to column. Arrange these results in subgroups of four and
    (a) Calculate acceptable values for $\bar{\bar{x}}$, $\bar{R}$, and control limits.
    (b) Calculate process capability.
    (c) Draw up $\bar{x}-R$ charts and plot all past data.
    (d) Comment on your findings.

Column: 1	2	3	4	5
0.37	0.44	0.53	0.28	0.32
0.33	0.44	0.44	0.40	0.32
0.49	0.50	0.40	0.43	0.34
0.46	0.59	0.35	0.30	0.34
0.39	0.38	0.40	0.42	0.31
0.44	0.42	0.26	0.46	0.31
0.20	0.42	0.28	0.34	0.30
0.52	0.37	0.31	0.36	0.31
0.45	0.52	0.05	0.30	0.32
0.10	0.45	0.34	0.29	0.24
0.41	0.47	0.33	0.33	0.25
0.32	0.18	0.35	0.33	0.25
0.35	0.50	0.25	0.30	0.31
0.32	0.52	0.29	0.32	0.36
0.29	0.68	0.32	0.27	0.32
0.23	0.25	0.26	0.31	0.34
0.31	0.59	0.32	0.30	0.31
0.14	0.49	0.29	0.28	0.36
0.37	0.59	0.29	0.32	0.48
0.39	0.52	0.34	0.31	0.31

Note: Start at the top of column 1 and work downward to the bottom; then move to the top of column 2 and repeat the process until all results have been tabulated.

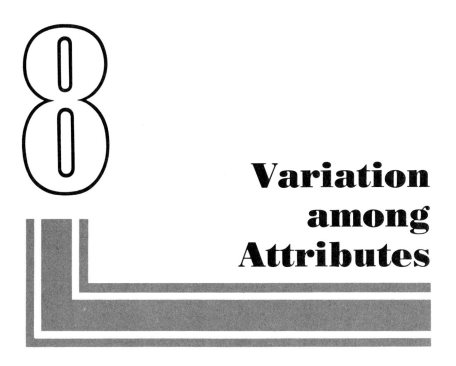

Variation among Attributes

8-1   DEFECTS AND DEFECTIVES

The terms "defect" and "defective" are used frequently when we are involved with attributes in quality control, and it is therefore important to note the distinction between the two. Defects are the faults or errors in an item which cause it to be unacceptable, and an unacceptable item may have one or more defects. The item which has the defect is described as being a defective item or, more commonly, simply as a "defective." The terms "reject" and "scrap" are also commonly used in place of "defective," but strictly speaking the word "scrap" should only be used where no form of rework or reclamation is possible.

8-2   WHOLE NUMBERS

When the quality characteristic which we wish to control is something which has to be counted rather than measured, we are involved with attributes rather than variables. We have seen that variables are characteristics which are measured on some kind of continuous scale and can have fractional values, but attributes are characteristics which an item either has or does not have, so attributes can only be counted in whole numbers.

For example, if we take a sample of 200 units from a large batch, we could find zero defectives or one, two, three or more defectives, but it will always be a whole number. There is no such thing as a fractional defective item. We cannot have one and a half defectives; the product is either acceptable or it is not. There is no in between condition.

Similarly, if we are looking for imperfections on a surface, we may find that there are no pinhole defects, or that there are one, two, three, or more pinholes. There can never be a fraction of a pinhole; one may be smaller than another, but it is still a pinhole.

8-3   GO, NO-GO INSPECTION

If we are controlling the diameter of a spindle which has to fit into a bushing, we may treat it as a variable, measure the diameters with a micrometer, and use $\bar{x} - R$ charts for control purposes. However, this may prove to be time consuming where large numbers are involved, so we may decide to do our inspection with a Go, No-Go gauge. Such a gauge would have two precision-ground holes, one which a spindle must be able to enter and the other which it must not enter, if it falls within the tolerance limits.

If the spindle will go into the Go hole but not into the No-Go hole, its diameter is within the specification, but if it will not go into the Go hole, it is too large, and if it will go into the No-Go hole, it is too small. Similarly, when it is a hole which is being inspected, we may use a plug gauge one end of which should be able to enter the hole (Go) and the other end not enter (No-Go) when the hole is within specification.

With gauges such as these we can sort the product into three categories, on-size, oversize, and undersize, or we may simplify things even further and classify the product as being either acceptable or reject. In either case we do not record the actual dimensions but simply count the number of rejected items in each sample or batch.

If reworking or custom fitting of off-sized items is not possible, we will take the simpler of these two approaches and simply count the number of rejected items and express them as a fraction or as a percentage of the number inspected. This is perhaps the more common approach and permits the use of the binomial distribution in analyzing the results.

8-4   PERCENT DEFECTIVE

Suppose that in a manufacturing operation we were drawing samples of 200 items at a time from larger batches of product. We would record the number of defectives found in each sample and express this as a fraction or as a percentage of the total number in the sample. For example, if we found three defectives, the fraction defective would be $\frac{3}{200}$ or 0.015. If we had continued with this process until we had collected 20 samples, then the results might look like those shown in Table 8-1. We have inspected a total of 4,000 items and

Table 8-1   RECORD OF FRACTION DEFECTIVE

Sample No.	No. of Defectives (r)	Fraction Defectives (p)
1	3	0.015
2	4	0.020
3	3	0.015
4	6	0.030
5	4	0.020
6	4	0.020
7	2	0.010
8	7	0.035
9	4	0.020
10	5	0.025
11	5	0.025
12	4	0.020
13	7	0.035
14	2	0.010
15	6	0.030
16	4	0.020
17	3	0.015
18	1	0.005
19	7	0.035
20	5	0.025
	$\sum r = 86$	$\sum p = 0.430$

Size of sample: $n = 200$.

found 86 of these to be defective, so we could make the mathematical statement

$$\text{Mean fraction defective } \overline{p} = \frac{\sum r}{\sum n}$$

$$= \frac{86}{4,000}$$

$$= 0.0215 \quad \text{or} \quad 2.15\%$$

However, we have used samples of equal size, so we could find $\overline{p}$ by averaging the fraction defective values and thus avoid the use of large numbers.

$$\text{Mean fraction defective } \overline{p} = \frac{\sum \overline{p}}{\text{number of samples}}$$

$$= \frac{0.43}{20}$$

$$= 0.0215 \quad \text{or} \quad 2.15\%$$

As we accumulate more and more values, $\overline{p}$ will approach the mean value for the system, and we could therefore say that, in the long run, we could expect to find 2.15% of the product to be defective. Or we could say that there would be a 0.0215 probability of finding a defective item. **The mean level of defectives is therefore also the probability of the occurrence of a defective.**

8-5   THE BINOMIAL DISTRIBUTION

In the analysis of the variation of attribute values from sample to sample, there are two distributions which are most commonly referred to. The *Poisson distribution* is used where there is a count of the number of defects in an infinite universe. For example, when we are counting small imperfections on a surface, the only theoretical limitation to the number which could occur would be the size of the defect relative to the size of the area. In other words, for all practical purposes the universe in which they occur is almost infinite.

The *binomial distribution*, on the other hand, is used when we are looking at only two possibilities: an item is either acceptable or it is not. This distribution, then, is the one which would be appropriate when looking at the results of any type of Go, No-Go inspection, and would therefore be applicable to the percent defective example given in the previous section.

The symbols n, r, and p, which have already been used, are found in the binomial equation and are defined as follows:

r = number of times an event occurs (i.e., number of items rejected)

n = number of trials (i.e., number of items inspected; *note that n is always greater than r*)

p = probability that the event will occur (i.e., a defective item will be found)

There are only two probabilities in the binomial distribution: the probability that an event will occur and the probability that it will not. These are two mutually exclusive events, and the sum of their probabilities (as seen in Section 4-2) must be unity. One or the other must alway happen. To take care of this other probability, we use the symbol q.

q = probability that the event will not occur (i.e., the item will be acceptable)

$q = 1 - p$

One other symbol is also used; the factorial, !. For example,

$$3! = 3 \times 2 \times 1$$

$$5! = 5 \times 4 \times 3 \times 2 \times 1$$

The binomial probability is written as $P(r|n, p)$, which reads "The probability of finding r, given n and p, and the equation is

$$P(r|n, p) = \frac{n!}{r!(n - r)!} \cdot p^r q^{(n - r)}$$

This formula can be used to find the probability of there being any specific number of defectives in a sample of any size. For example, if we were to take a sample of 50 items from a system which has a $\bar{p}$ value of 0.0125, what would be the probabilities of finding 0, 1, 2, 3, or 4 rejects?

$$P(0|50, 0.0125) = \frac{50!}{0! (50 - 0)!} \cdot 0.0125^0 \times 0.9875^{50}$$

$$= 1 \times 1 \times 0.533$$

$$= 0.533$$

$$P(1|50, 0.0125) = \frac{50!}{1!(50 - 1)!} \cdot 0.0125^1 \times 0.9875^{49}$$

$$= 50 \times 0.0125 \times 0.54$$

$$= 0.338$$

$$P(2|50, 0.0125) = \frac{50!}{2!(50 - 2)!} \cdot 0.0125^2 \times 0.9875^{48}$$

$$= 1,225 \times 0.0001562 \times 0.547$$

$$= 0.105$$

Similarly,

$$P(3|50, 0.0125) = 0.021$$

$$P(4|50, 0.0125) = 0.003$$

These values have been recorded as a histogram in Figure 8-1, and it can be seen immediately that the type of distribution is very much different from the normal distribution which we have previously studied.

8-5.1   Effect of the $\bar{p}$ Value

If the value for $\bar{p}$ were to be 0.05 instead of 0.0125 and we continued to take samples of 50, the results would be as follows:

$$P(0|50, 0.05) = 0.077$$

$$P(1|50, 0.05) = 0.203$$

$$P(2|50, 0.05) = 0.260$$

$$P(3|50, 0.05) = 0.220$$

$$P(4|50, 0.05) = 0.135$$

$$P(5|50, 0.05) = 0.066$$

$$P(6|50, 0.05) = 0.026$$

These results are shown as a histogram in Figure 8-2, and it can be

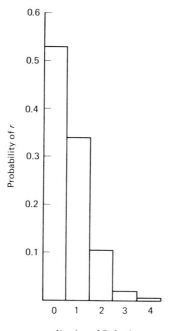

Figure 8–1   Probability of *r* Defectives
When $\bar{p} = 0.0125$, $n = 50$

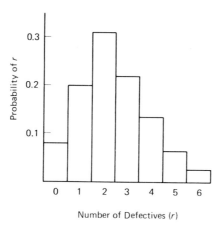

Figure 8–2   Probability of *r* Defectives When
$\bar{p} = 0.05$, $n = 50$

seen that although the distribution is still skewed it is beginning to take on a more normal appearance.

If we now consider the situation where the sample size remains the same, at 50, but the value for $\bar{p}$ is now 0.1, the probabilities of r now become

$$P(0|50, 0.1) = 0.005$$
$$P(1|50, 0.1) = 0.029$$
$$P(2|50, 0.1) = 0.078$$
$$P(3|50, 0.1) = 0.139$$
$$P(4|50, 0.1) = 0.181$$
$$P(5|50, 0.1) = 0.185$$
$$P(6|50, 0.1) = 0.154$$
$$P(7|50, 0.1) = 0.108$$
$$P(8|50, 0.1) = 0.064$$
$$P(9|50, 0.1) = 0.033$$
$$P(10|50, 0.1) = 0.015$$

The histogram of these results is shown in Figure 8-3, and a much closer approach to the normal distribution can now be seen. In fact, as $\bar{p}$ becomes larger still, the distribution becomes almost continuous, and the normal can be used as an approximation to the binomial.

8-5.2   Effect of Sample Size

There is another factor which we must consider, however, and that is the size of the sample. Common sense would tell us that as we

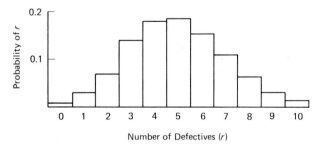

Figure 8–3   Probability of r Defectives When $\bar{p} = 0.10$, $n = 50$

Table 8-2 EFFECT OF SAMPLE SIZE ON BINOMIAL DISTRIBUTION WHEN $\bar{p} = 0.0125$

	Probability of r				
r	$n = 50$	$n = 100$	$n = 200$	$n = 400$	$n = 600$
0	0.533	0.284	0.081	0.007	0.0005
1	0.338	0.360	0.205	0.033	0.004
2	0.105	0.225	0.258	0.083	0.015
3	0.021	0.093	0.215	0.140	0.038
4	0.003	0.029	0.134	0.176	0.072
5	0.0004	0.007	0.067	0.177	0.109
6			0.027	0.147	0.137
7			0.010	0.105	0.147
8				0.065	0.138
9				0.036	0.115
10				0.018	0.086
11				0.008	0.058
12					0.036
13					0.021
14					0.011
15					0.005

take larger samples we are taking a larger proportion of the total population and hence creating a greater opportunity for larger numbers of defectives to be included in the sample. It would seem that it would be less and less likely that we would find zero defectives as we take larger and larger samples, and this is in fact the case.

Table 8-2 summarizes the probabilities of getting various numbers of defectives in samples of 50, 100, 200, 400, and 600, and it can be seen that the probabilities of finding zero defectives does in fact decline. Figures 8-4 through 8-7 show the histograms of these probabilities, and, when we compare them with Figure 8-1, we see that, as the probability of finding zero defectives declines, the highest probability (mode) moves farther and farther to the right. The distributions become less skewed and take on the typical appearance of a normal distribution.

We saw when we were studying variables that a relatively small subgroup could give a good indication of the condition of the process, but this is not the case with attributes.

A sampling plan should be able to indicate significant process changes for the better, as well as for the worse, but if there is a high probability of zero defectives, and we get zero defectives in the sample, we cannot tell if this is due to chance or to an assignable cause

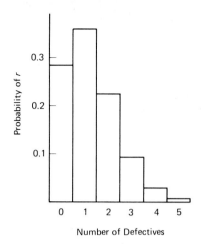

Figure 8-4 Probability of r Defectives
When $\bar{p} = 0.0125$, $n = 100$

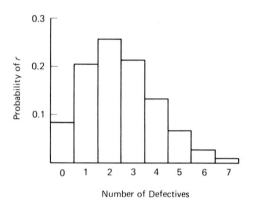

Figure 8-5 Probability of r Defectives When
$\bar{p} = 0.0125$, $n = 200$

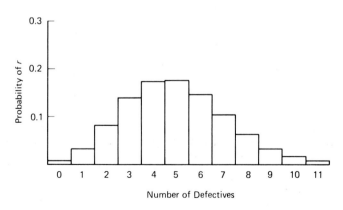

Figure 8-6 Probability of r Defectives When $\bar{p} = 0.0125$, $n = 400$

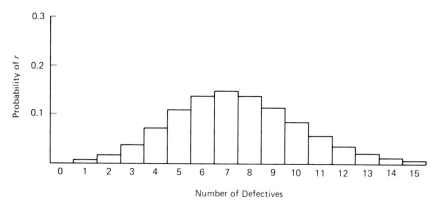

Figure 8-7   Probability of $\bar{r}$ Defectives When $\bar{p}$ = 0.0125, n = 600

which has improved the process. Larger samples are therefore necessary to ensure a low enough probability of obtaining no defectives
in a sample.

Figure 8-8 shows how the probability of having zero defectives
decreases with increasing sample size and with increasing fraction
defective, and it is obvious that it is only at low levels of fraction
defective that very large samples would be required. If we turn this
information around and plot the probabilities against the fraction
defective for three sample sizes, we obtain the curves shown in Figure 8-9. Here we can see again that as the fraction defective increases
the probability of finding no defectives in any sample decreases, and
that at any given level of defectives there is a lower probability with
the larger sample.

For example, at a process mean of 0.015 there is

1. A probability of 0.045 of finding no defectives in a sample of
   200.
2. A probability of 0.22 of finding no defectives in a sample of
   100.
3. A probability of 0.47 of finding no defectives in a sample of 50.

This type of relationship holds true until the curves blend into the
x axis. At this level of defectives a larger sample will have little
practical effect on the probability of not finding any defectives in
the sample. In general, however, a larger sample will be more sensitive to **improvements** in the process mean than will a smaller
sample.

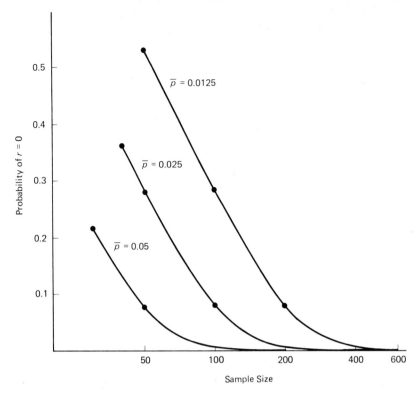

Figure 8–8 Probability of $r = 0$ for Three Process Means

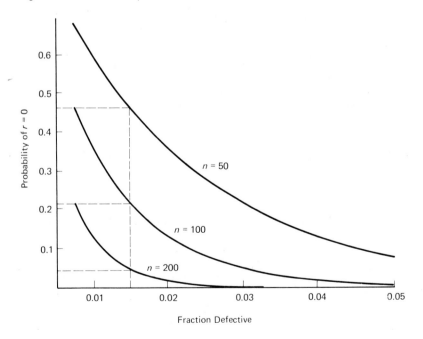

Figure 8–9 Probability of $r = 0$ for Three Sample Sizes

In Chapter 9 we will elaborate on the type of curve shown in Figure 8-9, and we will use these curves for much more detailed analyses of sampling plans. Table 8-3 contains the values used to plot the curves in Figures 8-8 and 8-9.

Table 8-3 PROBABILITY OF ZERO DEFECTIVES WITH VARIOUS SAMPLE SIZES AND PROCESS MEANS

$\bar{p}$	n	$P(0)$
0.0075	50	0.686
0.0075	100	0.471
0.0075	200	0.222
0.0075	300	0.105
0.0075	400	0.049
0.0125	50	0.533
0.0125	100	0.284
0.0125	200	0.081
0.0125	400	0.007
0.0125	600	0.001
0.0175	40	0.494
0.0175	50	0.414
0.0175	100	0.171
0.0175	200	0.029
0.0175	300	0.005
0.025	40	0.363
0.025	50	0.282
0.025	100	0.080
0.025	200	0.006
0.025	400	0.000
0.0325	40	0.267
0.0325	50	0.192
0.0325	100	0.037
0.0325	200	0.001
0.040	40	0.195
0.040	50	0.130
0.040	100	0.017
0.040	200	0.000
0.050	30	0.215
0.050	40	0.129
0.050	50	0.077
0.050	100	0.006

8-5.3   Cumulative Probabilities

The binomial distribution is not only used to determine the probability of finding a specific number of defectives but also the probabilities of finding "not more than" or "more than" some specific number. For example, in the case where $\bar{p} = 0.0125$, we may want to know the probability of getting not more than two defectives in a sample.

The probability of finding not more than two is the probability of finding zero, plus the probability of finding one, plus the probability of finding two. Stated another way, it is the probability of r being equal to or less than two. In this case we would have

$$\text{Probability of not more than two} = P(r \leq 2)$$
$$= P(0) + P(1) + P(2)$$
$$= 0.0533 + 0.338 + 0.105$$
$$= 0.976$$

That is, **in the long run,** 97.6% of the samples will contain not more than two defectives. Or, looking at it from the opposite point of view, only 2.4% will contain more than two defectives ($100 - 97.6 = 2.4$). Similarly,

$$P(r \leq 3) = 0.533 + 0.338 + 0.105 + 0.021$$
$$= 0.997$$

Or 99.7% will contain not more than three defectives. In other words, there is only a 0.003 probability (3 chances in 1,000) of a sample containing four or more defectives. Obviously, such information would be useful in determining whether or not an assignable cause was likely to have produced a change in the mean quality level of the process.

8-5.4   Calculation Problems

The calculations involved in binomial probabilities can be rather cumbersome, but some assistance can be obtained from published tables. Unfortunately, these tables are only of use when relatively small numbers are involved, as it is not common to find tables which list n values greater than 20.

The preprogrammed calculator is, once again, the answer to our computational problems. Not only does it give speed, but it permits the proper use of the binomial distribution where previously it might have been avoided or approximated. All the probability values given in this chapter were calculated with such an instrument.

8-6   THE p-CHART

We have already looked at the justification for the use of charts in the control of variables, and the same arguments hold true for the control of attributes. In the case of the Go, No-Go type of inspection, the appropriate chart is the p-chart, in which we plot either fraction defective or percent defective. Percent is often preferred as it gives a larger number, which more people seem to be able to conceptualize.

We must also calculate control limits, and when p is the variable, the *standard error of the percents,* or the standard error of the fraction defective, is the governing factor. It is found from the formula

$$\sigma_p = \sqrt{\frac{\overline{p}(1 - \overline{p})}{n}}$$

where σ_p = standard error of the fraction defective (or percent defective)

$\overline{p}$ = mean fraction or percent defective

n = sample size

If we take the values from Table 8-1, the calculation would be as follows:

$$\sigma_p = \sqrt{\frac{0.0215 \, (1 - 0.0215)}{200}}$$

$$= 0.0103 \quad \text{or} \quad 1.03\%$$

Just as control limits for variables were set at three standard errors of the mean, control limits for attributes in p-charts are set at three standard errors of the percent. The formulas are generally written as

$$\text{UCL} = \overline{p} + 3 \cdot \sqrt{\frac{\overline{p}(1 - \overline{p})}{n}}$$

$$\text{LCL} = \overline{p} - 3 \cdot \sqrt{\frac{\overline{p}(1 - \overline{p})}{n}}$$

In the preceding example, these equations would become

$$UCL = 0.0215 + 0.0308$$
$$= 0.0523 \quad \text{or} \quad 5.23\%$$
$$LCL = 0.0215 - 0.0308$$
$$= 0$$

Note that the LCL subtraction gives a negative number, but as it is impossible to have a negative amount of reject. we set the limit at zero. The values from Table 8-1 would give a chart such as that shown in Figure 8-10.

8-6.1   Effect of Sample Size

If the size of the sample and of the number of defectives in each sample were four times as great as those in Table 8-1, then the fraction or percent defective would be exactly the same as those in Table 8-1. The values are shown in Table 8-4, and once again we have

$$\bar{p} = \frac{\Sigma p}{\text{no. of samples}}$$

$$= \frac{0.43}{20}$$

$$= 0.0215$$

which is the same as for Table 8-1.

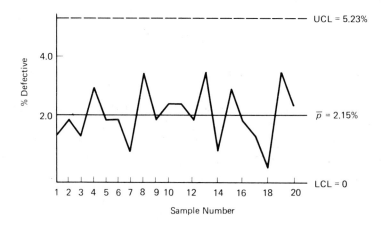

Figure 8–10 $\bar{p}$-chart for Table 8–1

Table 8-4   RECORD OF FRACTION DEFECTIVE:
SAMPLE SIZE $n = 800$

Sample No.	No. of Defectives (r)	Fraction Defective (p)
1	12	0.015
2	16	0.020
3	12	0.015
4	24	0.030
5	16	0.020
6	16	0.020
7	8	0.010
8	28	0.035
9	16	0.020
10	20	0.025
11	20	0.025
12	16	0.020
13	28	0.035
14	8	0.010
15	24	0.030
16	16	0.020
17	12	0.015
18	4	0.005
19	28	0.035
20	20	0.025
	$\sum r = 344$	$\sum p = 0.430$

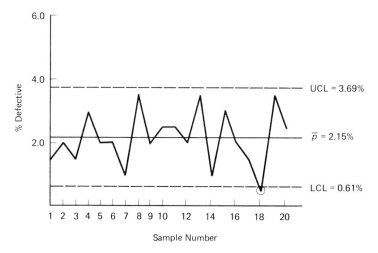

Figure 8–11 $\bar{p}$-chart for Table 8–3

However, we have already seen in Section 8-5.2 that a larger sample more closely approaches the Normal and is therefore likely to be more sensitive in indicating out-of-control conditions. Figure 8-11 shows that, **had the percentages remained the same,** one of the values would have been out of control.

The control limits from Table 8-4 data are calculated as follows:

$$UCL = \bar{p} + 3 \cdot \sqrt{\frac{\bar{p}(1 - \bar{p})}{n}}$$

$$= 0.0215 + 3 \cdot \cdot \sqrt{\frac{0.0215(0.9785)}{800}}$$

$$= 0.0215 + 0.0154$$

$$= 0.0369 \quad or \quad 3.69\%$$

$$LCL = \bar{p} - 3 \cdot \sqrt{\frac{\bar{p}(1 - \bar{p})}{n}}$$

$$= 0.0215 - 3 \cdot \sqrt{\frac{0.0215(0.9785)}{800}}$$

$$= 0.0215 - 0.0154$$

$$= 0.0061 \quad or \quad 0.61\%$$

It must be emphasized, however, that simply increasing the sample size by four times will not necessarily increase the defectives by four times. If the quality level remains the same, the probability of finding any particular number of defectives will change.

For example, if we take 2%, which is the most commonly occurring value in our comparison, we find that this is associated with 4 defectives in a sample of 200 or 16 defectives in a sample of 800. The associated probabilities are

$$P(4|200, 0.0215) = 0.195$$

$$P(16|800, 0.0215) = 0.096$$

There is a very much lower probability of obtaining 16 defectives in a sample of 800 than of finding 4 in a sample of 200, even though they both represent the same percentage defective. Even if we look at the cumulative probabilities, there is a lower probability of obtaining 16 or less in a sample of 800 than there is of obtaining 4 or

Table 8-5   RECORD OF FRACTION DEFECTIVE WITH VARIABLE SAMPLE SIZE

Sample No.	Sample Size	No. Defective	% Def.	$3\sigma_p$	UCL	LCL
1	840	18	0.021	0.0149	0.0355	0.0057
2	782	19	0.024	0.0154	0.0360	0.0052
3	726	17	0.023	0.0160	0.0366	0.0046
4	892	18	0.020	0.0144	0.0350	0.0062
5	764	18	0.024	0.0156	0.0362	0.0050
6	900	19	0.021	0.0144	0.0350	0.0062
7	914	15	0.016	0.0142	0.0348	0.0064
8	850	17	0.020	0.0148	0.0354	0.0058
9	800	15	0.019	0.0152	0.0358	0.0054
10	886	19	0.021	0.0145	0.0351	0.0061
11	838	20	0.024	0.0149	0.0355	0.0057
12	778	19	0.024	0.0154	0.0360	0.0052
13	928	18	0.019	0.0141	0.0347	0.0065
14	700	14	0.020	0.0163	0.0369	0.0043
15	718	14	0.019	0.0161	0.0367	0.0045
16	832	19	0.023	0.0149	0.0355	0.0057
17	920	19	0.021	0.0142	0.0348	0.0064
18	908	18	0.020	0.0143	0.0349	0.0063
19	884	17	0.019	0.0145	0.0351	0.0061
20	908	17	0.019	0.0143	0.0349	0.0063
$\sum n = 16,768$		$\sum r = 350$				

We can therefore expect that samples of different sizes will result in different charts for the same process. Because of this, where it is not possible to have samples of equal size, we do not draw continuous lines for the control limits, but recalculate control limits each time the sample size changes. This produces a staggered line, which rises and falls depending on sample size.

Under conditions where it is not practicable to have a constant sample size, the inspection results might be collected as in Table 8-5 and illustrated in Figure 8-12.

8-7   THE POISSON DISTRIBUTION

The Poisson Distribution is the one which is appropriate when we are counting the number of occurrences of an event in an infinite universe. It is therefore appropriate when we are counting such things as the number of defects on a surface or the number of acci-

Figure 8–12   Fraction Defective with Variable Sample Size

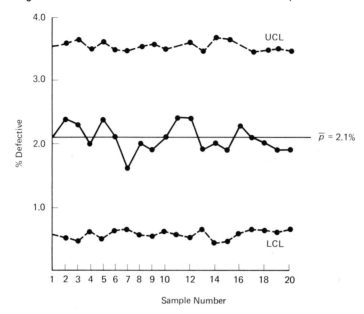

dents in a plant. The surface can be considered to be infinite relative to the size of the defect, and the times in which an accident did **not** occur can also be considered to be infinite.

The probability equation for the Poisson distribution is

$$P(r) = \frac{\mu^r e^{-\mu}}{r!}$$

$$= \frac{\mu^r}{r! \, e^{\mu}}$$

where r = number of occurrences of the event (i.e., number of defects); different symbols are used in most other publications, but r is used here to be consistent with the use of r in the binomial

$P(r)$ = probability of the event occurring r times (i.e., the probability of finding r defects)

μ (mu) = mean number of occurrences per unit of a given size

e = constant, 2.7183

For example, suppose that an enameled item is inspected for surface defects, and out of past production of 10,000 units 250 defects were found. The probability of finding a defect is found from

$$\overline{p} = \frac{\text{no. of defects}}{\text{no. inspected}}$$

$$= \frac{250}{10,000}$$

$$= 0.025$$

If we produce these units in batches of 200, we would be interested in knowing the probabilities of finding various numbers of defects in such batches. First, however, we must determine the mean number of occurrences of defects in a batch of this size, and it is simply the product of the probability of finding a defect and the sample size. That is,

$$\mu = n\overline{p}$$

which in our case becomes

$$\mu = 200 \times 0.025$$

$$= 5.0$$

(Note that, although r is always a whole number, μ is an average and may therefore have fractional values.)

If we now want to find the probability of there being two defects in a batch, we use the formula

$$P(2) = \frac{\mu^r}{r!e^\mu}$$

$$= \frac{5^2}{2!e^5}$$

$$= \frac{25}{2 \times 148.4}$$

$$= 0.084$$

That is, there is a 0.084 probability of finding two defects.

Similarly, the probability of finding three would be

$$P(3) = \frac{5^3}{3!\,e^5}$$

$$= \frac{125}{6 \times 148.4}$$

$$= 0.140$$

That is, there is a 0.14 probability of finding three defects. We could continue in this manner or, more conveniently, use a preprogrammed calculator to obtain the values for the other probabilities.

The Poisson is appropriate when $\overline{p}$ is small and the sample or universe is large. The mean number of defects is then dependent on sample size, and in the preceding case, where $\overline{p} = 0.025$,

$$\mu = 1 \text{ when } n = 40$$

$$\mu = 2 \text{ when } n = 80$$

$$\mu = 3 \text{ when } n = 120$$

$$\mu = 4 \text{ when } n = 160$$

$$\mu = 5 \text{ when } n = 200$$

$$\mu = 6 \text{ when } n = 240$$

and so on.

8-7.1   Effect of μ on the Poisson Distribution

If we calculate the probabilities of getting various r values for a range of μ values of from 1 to 6, we obtain the results shown in Table 8-6. The probabilities for μ values of 1, 2, 4, and 6 have been drawn as histograms and are shown in Figures 8-13 through 8-16, and we can see a trend toward a more normal distribution as the μ value increases. This increase in μ is, as we have seen, associated with an increase in n for any given value of $\overline{p}$. So we can say that as n and μ increase the distribution becomes less skewed and more normal in appearance. More correctly, it approaches the binomial, and the Poisson distribution is also known as Poisson's exponential binomial limit.

Table 8-6 EFFECT OF μ ON POISSON PROBABILITIES

			μ			
r	1	2	3	4	5	6
0	0.3679	0.1353	0.0498	0.0183	0.0067	0.0025
1	0.3679	0.2707	0.1494	0.0733	0.0337	0.0149
2	0.1839	0.2707	0.2240	0.1465	0.0842	0.0446
3	0.0613	0.1804	0.2240	0.1954	0.1404	0.0892
4	0.0153	0.0902	0.1680	0.1954	0.1755	0.1338
5	0.0031	0.0361	0.1008	0.1563	0.1755	0.1606
6	0.0005	0.0120	0.0504	0.1042	0.1462	0.1606
7	0.0001	0.0034	0.0216	0.0595	0.1044	0.1377
8	—	0.0009	0.0081	0.0298	0.0653	0.1033
9	—	0.0002	0.0027	0.0132	0.0363	0.0688
10	—	—	0.0008	0.0053	0.0181	0.0413
11	—	—	0.0002	0.0019	0.0082	0.0225
12	—	—	—	0.0006	0.0034	0.0113
13	—	—	—	0.0002	0.0013	0.0052
14	—	—	—	0.0001	0.0005	0.0022

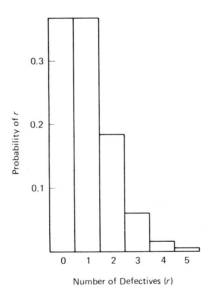

Figure 8–13 Probability of r Defectives When $\mu = 1$

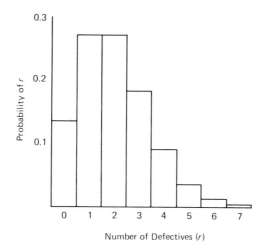

Figure 8–14 Probability of r Defectives When $\mu = 2$

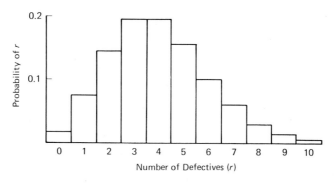

Figure 8–15 Probability of r Defectives When $\mu = 4$

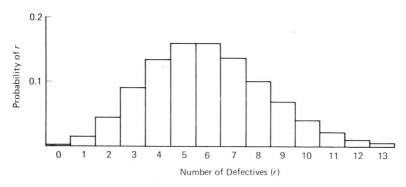

Figure 8–16 Probability of r Defectives When $\mu = 6$

The binomial calculations are much more cumbersome than those of the Poisson, and, in the past, this has resulted in the Poisson being used as an approximation to the binomial. Whether this will continue with the use of minicomputers and preprogrammed calculators remains to be seen. It has been particularly used where n is large, and hence the factorials and powers in the Binomial are also large. For example, if the fraction defective is 0.03, what is the probability of finding six defectives in a sample of 300?

1. *Using the binomial,*

$$P(6|300, 0.03) = \frac{300!}{6!(294!)} \cdot 0.03^6 \times 0.97^{294}$$

Such a case is beyond the limits of most binomial tables, and although canceling will reduce the factorials, it is still a lengthy calculation. It becomes

$$P(6|300, 0.03) = \frac{300 \times 299 \times 298 \times 297 \times 296 \times 295}{6 \times 5 \times 4 \times 3 \times 2 \times 1} \times$$

$$7.29 \times 10^{-10} \times 1.29 \times 10^{-4}$$

$$= \frac{6.93 \times 10^{14}}{720} \times 9.41 \times 10^{-14}$$

$$= 0.0906$$

2. *Using the Poisson,*

$$\mu = np = 300 \times 0.03 = 9$$

$$r = 6$$

$$P(6) = \frac{9^6}{6! \ 2.7183^9}$$

$$= \frac{531,441}{(6 \times 5 \times 4 \times 3 \times 2 \times 1) \times 8,103.57}$$

$$= \frac{531,441}{583 \times 10^6}$$

$$= 0.0911$$

The Poisson calculation is simpler and for all practical purposes gives the same result (0.091) as the binomial in this case. However, both calculations take less than 20 seconds on a preprogrammed calculator, so the justification for the Poisson is much less under these circumstances.

8-7.2   Cumulative Probabilities

We must be careful when first looking at Poisson distributions not to assume that there will always be a high probability of the occurrence of an individual event just because the r and μ values are the same, or are close. A look at Figures 8-13 through 8-16 shows that as μ increases in value the distributions become flatter at the same time as they become wider. This means that, although the **relative** probability within one distribution may be highest when $r = \mu$, the **absolute** probability declines with increasing r and μ. Table 8-7 and Figure 8-17 illustrate this characteristic.

However, in a similar way as with the binomial, we are frequently interested in knowing the probability of finding "more than" or "not more than" a certain number of defects per unit of production, and when we do this the probability of r becomes high. Table 8-8 and Figure 8-18 illustrate how the probability of r being equal to or less than μ increases in value, and we can see that this is indeed a high value and that it seems to tend toward a limiting value slightly greater than 0.5 as μ becomes larger and the distribution becomes less skewed.

Table 8-7   PROBABILITY OF r WHEN $r = \mu$

μ and r	$P(r)$
1	0.3679
2	0.2707
3	0.2240
4	0.1954
5	0.1755
6	0.1606
10	0.1251
15	0.1024
20	0.0888
30	0.0726
40	0.0629
50	0.0563
60	0.0514

Table 8-8   PROBABILITY OF r OR LESS WHEN $r = \mu$

μ and r	$P(r \leq \mu)$
1	0.7357
2	0.6767
3	0.6472
4	0.6289
5	0.6160
6	0.6062
10	0.5830
15	0.5681
20	0.5591
30	0.5484
40	0.5419
50	0.5375
60	0.5343
70	0.5317
80	0.5297

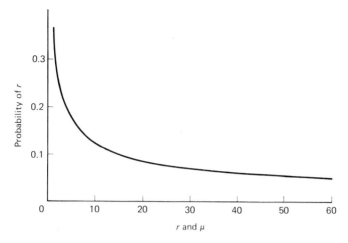

Figure 8–17   Probability of r When $\mu = r$

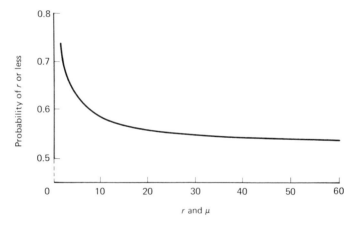

Figure 8–18   Probability of r or Less When $\mu = r$

More often, we are interested in cases more remote from the mean and, for example, if the mean number of defects is four, we might be interested in the probability of finding no more than two defects. The probability of finding no more than two defects is the same as the probability of finding two or less.

$$P\,(r \leq 2) = P(0) + P(1) + P(2)$$
$$= 0.0183 + 0.0733 + 0.1465$$
$$= 0.2381$$

Conversely, we may wish to know the probability of finding three or more defects. The probability that any event will occur is the sum of all the probabilities, or, unity, so the probability of three or more can be found from one minus the probability of two or less.

$$P\ (r \geq 3) = 1 - [P(0) + P(1) + P(2)]$$

$$= 1 - 0.2381$$

$$= 0.7619$$

Alternatively, the probability of three or more may be found by summing the various probabilities from three upward. The summation is stopped when the probability of a particular r value is so small as to be regarded as zero for all practical purposes. For example,

$$P\ (r \geq 3) = P(3) + P(4) + P(5) + P(6) + \ldots + P(14)$$

$$= 0.1954 + 0.1954 + 0.1563 + 0.1042 + 0.0595 + 0.0298$$
$$+ 0.0132 + 0.0052 + 0.0019 + 0.0006 + 0.0002 + 0.0001$$

$$= 0.7618$$

This is a more lengthy addition, so we would generally find the probability at the shorter end of the distribution and find the other by subtracting from unity.

Fortunately, cumulative tables exist, and where they go as high as a μ value of 25 (as in Appendix 7), they can have wide practical use. Where μ values exceed 25, it is necessary to make use of a computer.

8-8   THE c-CHART

When we are dealing with the number of defects in a unit, the appropriate chart for control purposes is called the c-chart. In this case, c denotes the actual number of defects in a unit, so this would be the equivalent of r in our formula. The average number of defects per unit is denoted by $\bar{c}$, so this would be the equivalent of μ in the formula. We should also note that, when the Poisson is used as an approximation of the binomial, $\bar{c}$ is interchangeable with $\bar{p}$.

For purposes of the c-chart, a "unit" may be an automobile, an airplane, or some other complex assembly where numbers of defects of various kinds are counted at final inspection; or it may be a subgroup of a constant size of somewhat smaller items in which the numbers of defects are counted. In all cases the subgroups must be uniform in that they must provide a relatively equal probability of the occurrence of a defect. If we mix products or processes with different μ values, the Poisson and hence the c-chart may no longer be appropriate.

8-8.1   Quality Improvement

The c-chart may be used on a continuing basis or it may be used temporarily as part of a quality improvement program by itself or in conjunction with p-charts. An example of this application may be found in the foundry industry, where a standard product is being manufactured and quality has fallen to an unacceptably low level.

Castings are prone to defects caused by inadequate properties in the molding sand and, for example, if there has been a change in supplier or loss of a knowledgeable technician, it is possible for the sand-preparation process to become technically out of control. If this should happen, the **number and severity** of sand-related defects could increase to the point where large numbers of castings have to be rejected. Sand-related defects may be so innocuous as to cause surface imperfections which only affect the appearance of the product, or they may be so severe as to cause major discontinuities in the structure of the metal. A typical inspection program will accept a certain number of minor surface defects but reject when the **number or severity** goes beyond some specified limit.

If p-charts were to be used alone in a quality-improvement program, it would not be unusual to find people easing up on their efforts as soon as the $\overline{p}$ value dropped to some acceptable level. However, a large number of surface defects might still exist, and unless c-charts were also in use this might go unnoticed.

As long as a large number of minor defects exist, the condition causing them has not been completely corrected, and, with the process still on the borderline, it could deteriorate rapidly. The use of c-charts would point out that, although a larger quantity of the production was acceptable, the probability of defects was still high and the program should be continued until $\overline{c}$ was also at an acceptable level.

8-8.2   c-Chart Control Limits

The probability equation for the Poisson is simpler than that for the binomial, but the standard deviation formula is even more so. The standard deviation for the Poisson is simply the square root of the mean number of defects: $\sigma_r = \sqrt{\mu}$ or, for cumulative samples, $\sigma_c = \sqrt{\bar{c}}$. Once again limits are set at plus or minus three standard deviations, and, because of the skewed nature of the distribution, it is not uncommon to find the lower control limit at zero.

For example, past records indicate that out or every 100 units produced we can expect to find an average of 9.6 defects. Thus

$$\bar{c} = 9.6$$

$$\sigma_c = \sqrt{\bar{c}} = 3.1$$

$$\text{UCL} = 9.6 + (3 \times 3.1) = 9.6 + 9.3 = 18.9$$

$$\text{LCL} = 9.6 - (3 \times 3.1) = 9.6 - 9.3 = 0.3$$

Had $\bar{c}$ been 9 or less, LCL would have been at zero.

Table 8-9 and Figure 8-19 indicate a situation where the high mean from past records was probably due to the fact that controls were exercised in a very sporadic manner. Where there is no formal quality-control function, we sometimes find that controls are alternately tightened and relaxed depending on the demands made by other responsibilities on the time of the person in charge. Under these circumstances the condition illustrated in Figure 8-19 would probably repeat itself over and over again.

Table 8-9   NUMBER OF DEFECTS PER HUNDRED UNITS

Batch No.	c	Batch No.	c
1	19	15	13
2	20	16	10
3	14	17	3
4	19	18	11
5	15	19	0
6	17	20	1
7	12	21	11
8	11	22	3
9	14	23	4
10	15	24	1
11	18	25	0
12	19	26	0
13	15	27	6
14	11	28	1

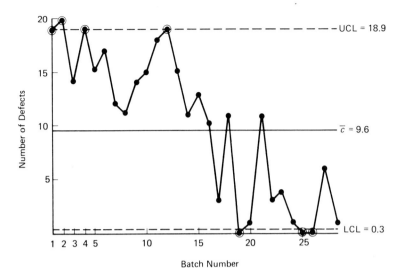

Figure 8-19   Number of Defects per Hundred Units

The out-of-control region with four results above the UCL and the region after tightened controls had taken effect both show ranges of c values which are much narrower than the expected range for a $\bar{c}$ of 9.6; if the controls can be continued, we could probably expect to establish a new mean at about 4.0 or less. Temporary relapses are not uncommon at the start of tightened controls, so batches 16, 18, and 21 may not be representative of possible future conditions. For this reason, caution should be exercised in the establishment of new control limits, and a much larger number of samples should be accumulated before this is done.

8-9   THE u-CHART

The use of the Poisson distribution need not be restricted to cases where sample or subgroup size is constant. In cases where 100% inspection is carried out, each day's production is likely to be different, and we can not therefore use c-charts.

We can, however, use the same principles but report the results as defects per unit or some multiple of units. Such defect information expressed as a rate rather than as an absolute number is plotted in an adaptation of the c-chart known as a u-chart. The symbols used are

$$n = \text{number of units}$$

$$c = \text{number of defects}$$

$$u = \frac{c}{n} \quad (\text{defects/unit})$$

$$\bar{u} = \frac{\sum c}{\sum n}$$

$$\text{UCL} = \bar{u} + 3\sqrt{\frac{\bar{u}}{n}}$$

$$\text{LCL} = \bar{u} - 3\sqrt{\frac{\bar{u}}{n}}$$

This means that instead of UCL and LCL being represented by a straight line, as in c-charts, they will require individual limit calculations for each subgroup plotted and will be represented by variable lines as in Figure 8-12.

8-9.1 Accident Frequency and u-Charts

It was stated earlier that the Poisson distribution was appropriate for the examination of accidents in a plant, and the u-chart is the one which is used for recording this information. Accidents are events which have a low but constant probability of occurring in an almost infinite universe. An accident may take less than a second to happen and, although it may be possible to count the number of "working" seconds in a day, the times available in which no accidents occur will be so large that they may be regarded as infinite for all practical purposes.

Industrial accidents are generally rated with regard to severity and frequency, and it is the frequency which may be plotted in a u-chart. Accident frequency is generally regarded as the **number** of lost-time accidents per working hour or some multiple of working hours. Usually, the value is so small per hour that it is difficult to conceptualize and is therefore multiplied by a constant, such as 200,000.

For example, if eight accidents occur in a month in which 140,000 hours are worked, the frequency would be 0.0000571 accidents per hour. This is obviously difficult to visualize in terms of whole numbers, but if we multiply by 200,000, it becomes 11.4 accidents/200,000 hours worked, and this makes more sense as an ac-

Table 8-10   LOST-TIME ACCIDENTS AND HOURS WORKED

Year	Month	Lost-Time Accidents	Hours Worked	Accident Frequency	$3\sigma_u$	UCL
1978	Jan.	2	32,300	12.4	26.3	38.7
	Feb.	2	26,500	15.1	29.0	41.4
	Mar.	2	25,200	15.9	29.8	42.2
	Apr.	0	33,000	0	26.0	38.4
	May	1	34,300	5.8	25.5	37.9
	Jun.	1	34,800	5.8	25.3	37.7
	Jul.	3	24,600	24.4	30.1	42.5
	Aug.	4	25,000	32.0	29.9	42.3
	Sep.	3	29,100	20.6	27.7	40.1
	Oct.	3	37,200	16.1	24.5	36.9
	Nov.	4	37,000	21.6	24.6	37.0
	Dec.	4	29,600	27.0	27.5	39.9
1979	Jan.	1	31,400	6.4	26.7	39.1
	Feb.	1	39,100	5.1	23.9	36.3
	Mar.	2	36,600	10.9	24.7	37.1
	Apr.	0	38,200	0	24.2	36.6
	May	1	37,600	5.3	24.4	36.8
	Jun.	1	39,000	5.1	23.9	36.3
	Jul.	3	36,200	16.6	24.8	37.2
	Aug.	3	31,400	19.1	26.7	39.1
	Sep.	0	20,500	0	33.0	45.4
	Oct.	0	39,700	0	23.7	36.1
	Nov.	4	41,200	19.4	23.3	35.7
	Dec.	4	34,900	22.9	25.3	37.7
1980	Jan.	0	39,100	0	23.9	36.3
	Feb.	1	44,200	4.5	22.5	34.9
	Mar.	4	38,500	20.8	24.1	36.5
	Apr.	1	46,200	4.3	22.0	34.4
	May	0	43,500	0	22.7	35.1
	Jun.	3	47,300	12.7	21.7	34.1
	Jul.	4	32,200	24.8	26.3	38.7
	Aug.	5	25,600	39.1	29.5	41.9
	Sep.	1	45,100	4.4	22.2	34.6
	Oct.	2	43,700	9.2	22.6	35.0
	Nov.	5	47,100	21.2	21.8	34.2
	Dec.	5	38,900	25.7	24.0	36.4

cident rate. The "unit" then becomes 200,000 hours and each month (i.e., sample) becomes a multiple or a fraction of that amount. In this example:

$$n = \frac{140,000}{200,000} = 0.70 \qquad \text{(this is the fraction of the}$$

$$\text{standard "unit")}$$

$$c = 8$$

$$u = \frac{8}{0.7} = 11.4 \qquad \text{(this is the rate/200,000 working}$$

$$\text{hours for the period)}$$

Accident frequency information is generally reported on a monthly basis, so it is necessary to go back in the records for two or three years to obtain a reasonably accurate value for $\overline{u}$. Table 8-10 shows such a review. From these records we obtain the following:

$$\text{Total number of lost-time accidents, } c = 80$$

$$\text{Total working hours} = 1,285,800$$

$$\text{Working hour units, } n = \frac{1,285,800}{200,000}$$

$$= 6.43$$

$$\text{Mean accident rate per unit, } \overline{u} = \frac{80}{6.43}$$

$$= 12.4$$

Using this value for $\overline{u}$, we now calculate three standard deviations and hence UCL for each individual month. Taking January 1978 as an example, the calculations are as follows:

$$n \quad = \frac{32,300}{200,000}$$

$$= 0.1615$$

$$3\sigma \quad = 3 \sqrt{\frac{\overline{u}}{n}}$$

$$= 3 \sqrt{\frac{12.4}{0.1615}}$$

$$= 3 \times 8.76$$

$$= 26.3$$

$$UCL = \overline{u} + 3\sigma$$

$$= 12.4 + 26.3$$

$$= 38.7$$

$$LCL = \overline{u} - 3\sigma$$

$$= 12.4 - 26.3$$

$$= 0$$

Note that 3σ is greater than $\overline{u}$ in each case, so LCL is zero throughout the period.

Figure 8-20 is the u-chart for the three-year period, and it can be seen that none of the values are **statistically** out of control. However, we can see at a glance that the value for August 1980 is extremely close to the UCL, and we must ask ourselves if this means that there is likely to be an assignable cause which could be associated with this result or if it could be expected by chance alone.

Figure 8-18 shows us that at a μ, or $\overline{u}$, value of 12.4 the distribution is not uniform and that more than half of the time we will obtain values which are less than μ, or $\overline{u}$. In other words, less than half the time the values will be greater than $\overline{u}$, and an UCL set at three standard deviations is therefore only a guide and does not give the clear-cut information on probability that we found with the normal distribution.

We must therefore calculate the probability of that frequency occurring in the sample size (hours worked) found in that month.

$$\text{Lost-time accidents, } c = 5$$

$$\text{Hours worked} = 25,600$$

$$n = \frac{25,600}{200,000}$$

$$= 0.128$$

$$u = \frac{5}{0.128}$$

$$= 39.1$$

The average frequency is 12.4 accidents per 200,000 working hours, but the plant did not work a whole unit, so the expected average number of accidents would be somewhat less.

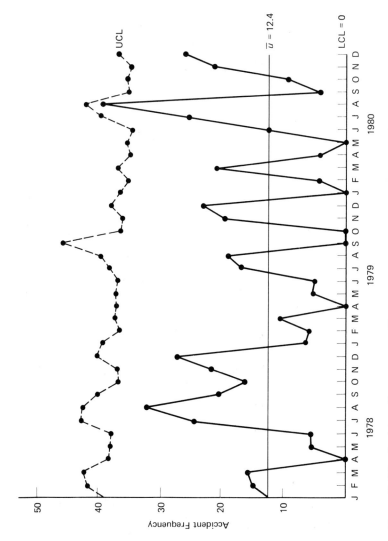

Figure 8–20 Accident Frequency u-Chart

Expected accidents (μ for sample) = universe average $\times$ sample size

$$= 12.4 \times 0.128$$

$$= 1.59$$

This is a one-tailed risk, similar in some ways to the risk of a variable being above specification, so we are not just interested in the probability of having five accidents but of having five or more. The probability of having five or more accidents when the mean expected number is 1.59 is only 0.0231, found from the Poisson probability equation, and

$$P(c \geq 5) = P(5) + P(6) + P(7) + P(8) + P(9)$$

$$= 0.0173 + 0.0046 + 0.0010 + 0.0002 + 0.0000$$

$$= 0.0231$$

That is, in the long run, we can expect this number of accidents only 2.3% of the time or only once in 43 months. Only 36 months have been examined, however, so there would seem to be reasonable grounds to doubt that the high frequency experienced in this month was due to chance alone. Besides, we are not dealing here with some industrial product, we are dealing with human suffering and perhaps even life, and under these circumstances we should be prepared to look for assignable causes at much lower levels of confidence than were previously established.

Instead of calculating upper and lower control limits, we could calculate the probabilities of the numbers of accidents being **at or beyond** the actual number found and tabulate them as in Table 8-11. If we then say that in the case of accidents we are prepared to look for assignable causes when the probability is less than 0.1, we can identify those with a low probability of occurring because of being either extremely low or extremely high.

Less than 0.1 probability of being at experienced value, or lower		Less than 0.1 probability of being at experienced value, or higher	
April 1979	(0.094)	August 1978	(0.072)
October 1979	(0.085)	August 1980	(0.023)
January 1980	(0.089)	December 1980	(0.097)
May 1980	(0.062)		

If we now examine the plant circumstances surrounding the low months and those surrounding the high months, we have a much better chance of finding distinguishing features which will be

Table 8-11 ACCIDENT PROBABILITIES

Year	Month	Lost-Time Accidents (c)	Average Expected Accidents	P(c)
1978	Jan.	2	2.00	0.6767
	Feb.	2	1.64	0.4879
	Mar.	2	1.56	0.4621
	Apr.	0	2.05	0.1287
	May	1	2.13	0.3720
	Jun.	1	2.16	0.3644
	Jul.	3	1.53	0.1987
	Aug.	4	1.55	0.0721
	Sep.	3	1.80	0.2694
	Oct.	3	2.31	0.4066
	Nov.	4	2.29	0.1986
	Dec.	4	1.84	0.1152
1979	Jan.	1	1.95	0.4197
	Feb.	1	2.42	0.3041
	Mar.	2	2.27	0.6040
	Apr.	0	2.37	0.0935
	May	1	2.33	0.3240
	Jun.	1	2.42	0.3041
	Jul.	3	2.24	0.3880
	Aug.	3	1.95	0.3098
	Sep.	0	1.27	0.2808
	Oct.	0	2.46	0.0854
	Nov.	4	2.55	0.2532
	Dec.	4	2.16	0.1728
1980	Jan.	0	2.42	0.0889
	Feb.	1	2.74	0.2415
	Mar.	4	2.39	0.2192
	Apr.	1	2.86	0.2211
	May	0	2.70	0.0621
	Jun.	3	2.93	0.5609
	Jul.	4	2.00	0.1429
	Aug.	5	1.59	0.0231
	Sep.	1	2.80	0.2311
	Oct.	2	2.71	0.4912
	Nov.	5	2.92	0.1715
	Dec.	5	2.41	0.0971

of use in an accident-prevention program. As the safety slogan says, "Accidents do not happen, they are caused." But their causes are so complex, being environmental, physiological, and psychological, that it is not easy to identify them. Probability theory does not provide guarantees, but it does provide a rational approach which is much more likely to be successful than if we examine each accident as though it were an individual incident existing on an island by itself.

QUESTIONS AND PROBLEMS

1. Define the terms "defect" and "defective."

2. Describe "Go, No-Go" inspection.

3. What value is used for the probability of there being a defective in a process?

4. Under what circumstances it is appropriate to use the binomial distribution?

5. Under what circumstances is it appropriate to use the Poisson distribution?

6. Draw a histogram to illustrate the distribution of 0, 1, 2, 3, 4, 5, and 6 rejects when the process mean is running at 2.0% defective and the sample size is 200.

7. Draw a histogram to cover the same cumulative probability as was found in question 6, but using a sample size of 400.

8. If a process is running at 1% defective and samples of 100 are being used, explain why we cannot say that there is an improvement in the process if we find no defectives in a sample.

9. What effect on the binomial distribution do the following have: (a) sample size; (b) mean fraction defective?

10. Illustrate with an example one reason why the Poisson distribution is used as an approximation to the binomial.

11. When $\mu = 6$, what are the probabilities of finding (a) two or less defects; (b) ten or more defects?

12. Sketch an approximate graph to illustrate what happens to the probability of finding r defects when $r = \mu$.

13. Under what circumstances might the Poisson distribution and c-charts be (a) inappropriate; (b) used on a temporary basis?

14. When would a u-chart be used instead of a c-chart?

15. Describe the steps you might go through to analyze the accident-frequency statistics for a plant or division.

16. In what way is the Poisson distribution affected by changes in μ?

17. The following numbers of defective units were found in 25 consecutive samples of 400 units: 18, 9, 12, 16, 18, 8, 14, 14, 15, 18, 13, 10, 14, 23, 18, 16, 12, 16, 10, 1, 0, 5, 11, 14, 10. Tabulate the results, calculate control limits, and draw up an appropriate p-chart.

18. The accident-frequency records for a plant over the past two years are shown in the following table. Prepare a u-chart for these and future values, and discuss the probability of finding assignable causes for both high and low accident rates in specific months.

Year No.	Month	Lost-Time Accidents	Hours Worked
1	Jan.	5	27,000
	Feb.	1	36,700
	Mar.	5	33,700
	Apr.	5	38,400
	May	1	37,000
	Jun.	2	23,300
	Jul.	10	34,000
	Aug.	7	25,100
	Sep.	5	40,400
	Oct.	6	49,200
	Nov.	4	42,200
	Dec.	6	47,600
2	Jan.	3	28,900
	Feb.	4	47,400
	Mar.	2	34,600
	Apr.	1	35,500
	May	2	39,300
	Jun.	4	21,500
	Jul.	8	36,200
	Aug.	9	31,800
	Sep.	3	28,000
	Oct.	1	28,400
	Nov.	3	45,900
	Dec.	6	46,300

Acceptance Sampling

9-1 ACCEPT OR REJECT

In Section 8-6 we looked at a case where the average fraction defective ($\bar{p}$) was 0.0215, and with a sample size of 200 this gave an upper control limit of 0.0523 and a lower control limit of zero. That is,

$$\bar{p} = 0.0215$$

$$\sigma_p = \sqrt{\frac{\bar{p}(1 - \bar{p})}{n}}$$

$$= \sqrt{\frac{0.0215(1 - 0.0215)}{200}}$$

$$= 0.01026$$

$$3\sigma_p = 0.0308$$

$$\bar{p} + 3\sigma_p = 0.0523$$

If we accept the approximation that 99.7% of all results will fall between these limits, we can then say that by chance alone we will

183

occasionally find ten defectives in a sample of 200. Eleven defectives would exceed our accepted level of probability, however, and we could expect to find an assignable cause for such a variation. That is,

$$\text{Upper limit of defectives in sample} = (\text{UCL})n$$

$$= 0.0523 \times 200$$

$$= 10.46$$

and $10 < 10.46 < 11$.

If we now decided that, if we drew a random sample of 200 from a lot and found ten or less defectives, we would accept the entire lot, but that if we found eleven or more we would reject the lot, we would have an acceptance sampling plan. It may have been arrived at in a somewhat unconventional manner, but it is a sampling plan. This plan would be described by

$$n = 200$$

$$c = 10$$

where n = sample size
         c = acceptance number (the largest number of defectives in the sample which will still allow the lot to be accepted)

Similarly, for a sample size of 800, a $\bar{p}$ of 0.0215, and an upper control limit of 0.0369,

$$\text{Upper limit of defectives in sample} = (\text{UCL})n$$

$$= 0.0369 \times 800$$

$$= 29.52$$

and we would accept the lot if we found 29 defectives in the sample, but reject it if we found 30. That is, $29 < 29.52 < 30$, and $n = 800$, $c = 29$.

All single sampling plans are described in part by their sample size and acceptance number. That is, for a sample of a given size the entire lot from which it is drawn will be accepted if the number of defectives is less than the acceptance number. If the number of defectives is greater than the acceptance number, the entire lot will be rejected.

Rejection does not necessarily mean that the items will all be scrapped. Where costs permit, it may simply mean that the lot is given 100% inspection. Similarly, the defective items themselves may be scrapped or reworked depending on the relative costs of replacement and reworking.

9-2   PROBABILITY OF ACCEPTANCE

The two sampling plans described in Section 9-1 might be acceptable under some circumstances, but the quality-control practitioner would want to have more information than simply the n and c values. One piece of information which we would like to have would be the probability of acceptance of various levels of rejects which we might encounter as the process fluctuates in a regular manner.

In Section 1-9 we examined the fact that all industrial processes have some particular quality level at which process and reject costs are minimized. This level we called the optimum quality of conformance, and it is at this level that we would hope to operate (that is, where optimum quality of conformance equals $\bar{p}$). In acceptance sampling terminology, where a plan has been designed by a manufacturer for internal use, this would also be known as the acceptable quality level, or AQL. That is,

$$\text{Optimum quality of conformance} = \bar{p} = \text{AQL}$$

This is what we would hope to have, but for a variety of reasons this equality may not always exist. There may have been an upward shift in $\bar{p}$, or an AQL may have been specified by a customer without regard to the existing level of mean percent defectives.

Now, if we were to conduct 100% inspection and this inspection were to be 100% effective, only two probabilities would be involved. There would be a probability of 1.0, or certainty, of accepting all lots where the percentage defectives was up to the acceptable quality level, and a probability of zero of accepting any lots where the percentage exceeded the acceptable quality level.

Such a condition could be represented graphically as in Figure 9-1, where a horizontal line at a Pa (probability of acceptance) value of 1.0 extends from a p value of zero to a p value of 2.15%, representing the certainty of accepting all lots with rejects up to the AQL. The line then drops vertically to a Pa value of zero and horizontally on to infinity, representing the certainty of no lots being accepted where the p value exceeds 2.15%.

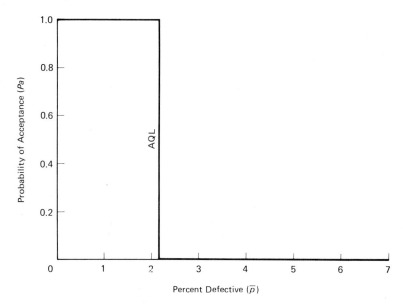

Figure 9–1   Probability of Acceptance with 100% Inspection

This, of course, is not practicable, as 100% inspection is not sampling, and sampling does not involve certainty. When we draw samples, we assume some risks. We assume the risk of rejecting a lot that should have been accepted and of accepting a lot that should have been rejected. By chance alone the **sample** may sometimes contain a disproportionately high number of defectives, and the **lot** may be rejected because the c value was exceeded, when in fact the lot should have been accepted. On other occasions, by chance alone, the sample may contain a disproportionately small number of defectives and the lot be accepted, when in fact the quality level was such that it should have been rejected. The question then arises as to what probabilities would exist in the plan which we have devised.

In Figure 9-1 the AQL is shown as the level below which all lots are accepted and above which all lots are rejected, but if the AQL were also to be $\bar{p}$, this would be somewhat unrealistic. By definition, a mean is a position of central tendency so that there should be results above as well as below this value, and if we are to be practical about this matter, there should be **some** degree of probability of accepting **some** of the results which are **above** AQL. We can find these probability/percent defective relationships for any sampling plan by drawing its operating characteristic curve.

9-3   OPERATING CHARACTERISTIC CURVE

The operating characteristic curve, or OC curve, describes in graphical form the probabilities associated with a particular sampling
plan. It is prepared by plotting individual percent defective values
against their corresponding probabilities of acceptance. Figure 9-1
is the theoretically "ideal" OC curve.

9-3.1   Drawing the OC Curve

We have already seen that the Poisson is a good approximation of
the binomial when p is small and n is large, and we take advantage
of this in our methodology. Appendix 7 shows the cumulative probabilities of c or less occurrences for various values of μ, and these
are plotted against their respective p values.

We first look in the Poisson cumulative tables under the acceptance number, which in our first example is 10. Enough probability values are **selected** so as to ensure the drawing of a smooth
curve. The appropriate np value for each is divided by the sample
size (200 in this case), and this gives the p coordinate for each Pa.
The values are tabulated for convenience.

Pa	np	p
0.990	4.8	0.024
0.982	5.2	0.026
0.949	6.2	0.031
0.871	7.4	0.037
0.706	9.0	0.045
0.521	10.5	0.0525
0.402	11.5	0.0575
0.252	13.0	0.065
0.145	14.5	0.0725
0.118	15.0	0.075
0.049	17.0	0.085
0.030	18.0	0.090

The Pa values are plotted against their corresponding p values, and
a curve such as that in Figure 9-2 is obtained. We can now see
graphically the varying probabilities of acceptance of lots, containing
up to ten defectives, as the process percent defective ranges from 0
to 9%. Each sample plan has its own OC curve, and we can compare
the effectiveness of sample plans by comparing their OC curves.

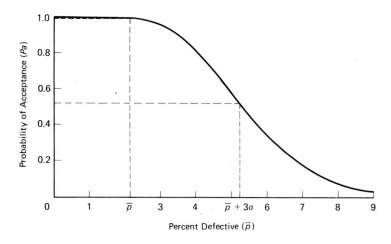

Figure 9–2   OC Curve for the Plan $n = 200$, $c = 10$

When we examine Figure 9-2, we can see that while it provides almost certainty of accepting lots when the p value corresponds with $\bar{p}$, it provides a probability of 0.52 of accepting lots at the top end of the range which we were prepared to accept $(\bar{p} + 3\sigma)$. This is much too high a probability, as it means that we will be accepting lots with **more** than ten defectives 48% of the times that they occur, and the plan will therefore not be sensitive to upward shifts in the process average.

This Pa of 0.52 may seem to be rather high considering our method of selection, but it must be remembered that we found a μ value and then substituted it for an r. If we go back to Section 8-7, the formula for mean number of defectives was $\mu = n\bar{p}$. We used $(\bar{p} + 3\sigma)$ in place of $\bar{p}$, so what we found was a mean number of defectives (μ), but we used this in place of r (or c) in the Poisson equation. The OC curve has shown this up, and our method of selecting a c number has therefore proved to be inadequate.

Without the OC curve our plan seemed to have a reasonable justification, but with the OC curve we see that this is not the case. The plan does not discriminate effectively enough between "good" and "bad" lots. In fact, when the process is running at as high as 7.6% defectives, we would be accepting lots 10% of the time. We must therefore set about selecting a plan in some other manner.

9-4   DESIGNING THE SAMPLE PLAN

If we have accepted the fact that by chance alone we will occasionally have reject values which are three standard deviations above the mean, we can still use this as the maximum level which we are prepared to accept. The question which remains is, how often can we tolerate such a level? It is obvious that 52% is much too high and that some subjective judgment may be involved here.

General practice is to use a probability of 0.10 for accepting lots at the maximum level which we can tolerate. We give this probability the symbol β (beta) and call it the *consumer's risk*. We call the quality at this level the *lot tolerance percent defective* (LTPD) or *lot tolerance fraction defective* (LTFD), depending on which method of reporting we use.

The lot tolerance percent defective may be arrived at by a method such as the one which we have used, or it may be arrived at by comparing the costs of various levels of inspection with the costs involved when reject items find their way into the production system. Lot tolerance percent defective might then be set by the maximum cost of rejects which we could tolerate at some subsequent stage in production. So, if we now say that we are only prepared to accept 5.23% defectives 10% of the time, we could retain a sample size of 200 and find the appropriate value for c by a process of elimination.

Appendix 7 shows the cumulative probabilities of c or less occurrences for varying values of μ, but we can also work backward in the table and find the μ values for varying values of c at constant probabilities. We know that μ is the average or expected number of occurrences and that this is dependent on the sample size and the mean percent defective.

$$\mu = n\bar{p}$$

$$\therefore \bar{p} = \frac{\mu}{n}$$

We will look in the tables for the μ value which corresponds to our specified probability of acceptance under a series of c values. Having fixed on our sample size, we can now calculate $\bar{p}$ for each value of c, and the appropriate acceptance number will be the one which gives the p value closest to LTFD. Unfortunately, the tables rarely display probabilities exactly at the value which we desire to use, so it is necessary to use interpolation.

9-4.1   Interpolating in the Poisson Cumulative Tables

Under a c value of zero we find that there is a Pa value of 0.111 and one of 0.091. The value which we need is between these two, so we use the following procedure:

	Pa		μ
	0.111		2.2
	0.091		2.4
Difference	0.020	Difference	0.2

Our desired value is 0.10, and we must find the difference between this and one of the given values.

$$
\begin{array}{r}
0.111 \\
0.100 \\
\hline
\text{Difference} \quad 0.011
\end{array}
$$

That is, 0.10 is 0.011/0.020 or $\frac{11}{20}$ of the numerical distance from 0.111 to 0.091. We then find the same fraction of the numerical distance from 2.2 to 2.4 and add this to 2.2.

$$\frac{11}{20} \times 0.2 = 0.11$$

and $\mu = 2.2 + 0.11$
$\quad\quad = 2.31$

Hence, when $c = 0$ and $Pa = 0.10$, $\mu = 2.31$. Similarly, when $c = 1$,

	Pa		μ
	0.107		3.8
	0.092		4.0
Difference	0.015	Difference	0.2

Our desired value is $\frac{7}{15}$ of the numerical distance from 3.8 to 4.0 and,

$$\frac{7}{15} \times 0.2 = 0.09$$

$$\mu = 3.8 + 0.09 = 3.89$$

Table 9–1 MEAN NUMBER OF OCCURRENCES
WHEN $\alpha = 0.05$ AND $\beta = 0.10$

	μ or $n\bar{p}$	
c or r	Pa = 0.95	Pa = 0.10
0	0.052	2.31
1	0.354	3.89
2	0.819	5.33
3	1.36	6.68
4	1.97	8.00
5	2.61	9.30
6	3.28	10.54
7	3.98	11.79
8	4.69	13.00
9	5.42	14.21
10	6.18	15.44
11	6.93	16.64
12	7.69	17.81
13	8.47	18.96
14	9.24	20.15
15	10.03	21.32
16	10.81	22.49
17	11.62	23.64
18	12.43	24.78
19	13.22	25.91
20	14.06	27.05

By means of this method, values for μ at a constant Pa of 0.10 have been found for a series of c values and for convenience have been tabulated under $Pa = 0.10$ in Table 9-1. Should any other Pa be desired, it would be necessary to use the preceding procedure.

9-4.2 The Process of Elimination

If we start the process at a c of four, we have $c = 4$, np (at $Pa = 0.10$) $= 8.00$, and $p = \frac{8}{200} = 0.040$. This p value is below the value which we are aiming for, so we must continue the process.

c	np (At $Pa = 0.10$)	p (Calculated)
5	9.3	0.047
6	10.54	0.0527

We were aiming for a p value of 0.0523, so the value at a c of six is closer to this than the value at a c of five. That is,

	0.0523		0.0527
	0.0470		0.0523
Difference	0.0053	Difference	0.0004

We will therefore examine the plan, $n = 200$, $c = 6$, and our table of values for drawing the OC curve will be as follows:

Pa	np	p
0.995	2.0	0.010
0.976	2.8	0.014
0.955	3.2	0.016
0.909	3.8	0.019
0.791	4.8	0.024
0.702	5.4	0.027
0.511	6.6	0.033
0.450	7.0	0.035
0.207	9.0	0.045
0.130	10.0	0.050
0.079	11.0	0.055
0.035	12.5	0.063

Figure 9-3 shows the OC curve obtained from these values, and we can see that it meets our specified requirement for LTPD. Unfortunately, the top of the graph has become more rounded, and this has dropped the probability of accepting lots at the process mean from close to 1.0 down to approximately 0.85. This means that the value which will tend to occur most often will only bring about acceptance 85% of the time. Most people would consider that this is not high enough. In fact, the generally accepted level is 95%. That is, when the process is running at the acceptable quality level, we would like to be accepting lots 95% of the time.

The probability of accepting at the AQL is generally referred to in its converse form as the probability of rejecting lots at the AQL, that is, lots that should have been accepted. It is given the symbol α (alpha) and is called the *producer's risk*.

We now have two pairs of coordinates for two key points on the OC curve:

α risk at AQL

β risk at LTPD

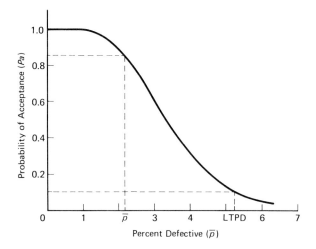

Figure 9–3   OC Curve for the Plan $n = 200$, $c = 6$

We arrived at $n = 200$, $c = 6$ by holding n constant at its predetermined value and finding the c value which met the LTPD specification, and it seems likely that if we did this in reverse we would not be any more successful (i.e., if we held n constant and found the c value which met the AQL specification). Another approach must therefore be considered.

Instead of holding one factor constant, we will leave both n and c free and select the plan which comes closest to meeting both AQL and LTPD requirements. The specification which we must meet is

$$\alpha = 0.05 \ (Pa = 0.95), \quad AQL = 2.15\% \ (or \ 0.0215)$$

$$\beta = 0.10, \quad LTPD = 5.23\% \ (i.e., LTFD = 0.0523)$$

Starting with a c of zero, we find μ in Table 9-1 under $Pa = 0.95$.

$$\mu = np = 0.052$$

$$\therefore 0.0215n = 0.052$$

$$\therefore n = \frac{0.052}{0.0215}$$

$$= 2.42$$

At a c of zero and $Pa = 0.10$, $np = 2.31$. We now substitute the calculated value of n in the equation and find

$$p = \frac{2.3}{2.42}$$

$$= 0.950$$

The calculated value of p at a probability of acceptance of 0.10 must come close to the specified p of 0.0523 in order to be acceptable. In this case 0.950 is far removed from 0.0523, so we must try again at a different c value.

When $c = 4$ and $Pa = 0.95$,

$$np = 1.97$$

$$\therefore n = \frac{1.97}{0.0215}$$

$$= 91.6$$

When $c = 4$ and $Pa = 0.10$,

$$np = \frac{8.00}{91.6}$$

$$= 0.087$$

This is much closer to 0.0523 than the previous calculated value, but it is still not close enough so we will now try a c of five.

When $c = 5$ and $Pa = 0.95$,

$$np = 2.61$$

$$\therefore n = \frac{2.61}{0.0215}$$

$$= 121.4$$

When $c = 5$ and $Pa = 0.10$,

$$np = 9.30$$

$$\therefore p = \frac{9.30}{121.4}$$

$$= 0.0766$$

This is still not close enough to 0.0523, so we must continue with the process. Generally, we set up our calculations in tabular form in order to have the results in a more organized manner; in the present case the table and results would be as follows:

c	np (Pa = 0.95)	Calculated n	np (Pa = 0.1	Calculated p
0	0.052	2.42	2.31	0.950
4	1.97	91.6	8.00	0.087
5	2.61	121.4	9.30	0.077
6	3.28	152.6	10.54	0.069
7	3.98	185.1	11.79	0.064
8	4.69	218.1	13.00	0.060
9	5.42	252.1	14.21	0.0564
10	6.18	287.4	15.44	0.0537 > LTFD
11	6.93	322.3	16.64	0.0516 < LTFD

The last two results are close to 0.0523, so we check to see which is the closer.

At $c = 10$,

$$\text{Deviation from aimed-at value} = 0.0537 - 0.0523$$

$$= 0.0014$$

At $c = 11$,

$$\text{Deviation from aimed-at value} = 0.0523 - 0.0516$$

$$= 0.0007$$

The p value when $c = 11$ is the closer of the two, and the plan which meets the specification is therefore

$$n = 322, \qquad c = 11$$

Figure 9-4 is the OC curve for this plan, and the tabulated values for drawing the curve are as follows:

Pa	np	p
0.990	5.4	0.017
0.980	6.0	0.019
0.849	8.5	0.026
0.752	9.5	0.0295
0.579	11.0	0.034
0.406	12.5	0.039
0.304	13.5	0.042
0.055	18.0	0.056
0.021	20.0	0.062

We can see that we now have a plan which meets the requirements of our specification and in addition is steeper than either of the other two.

The steeper the OC curve, the more closely it approaches the "ideal" shown in Figure 9-1, the more it discriminates between ac-

Figure 9–4   OC Curve for the Plan $n = 322$, $c = 11$

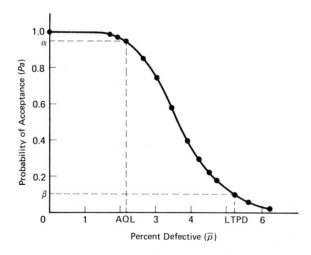

ceptable and unacceptable lots. We say that the $n = 322$, $c = 11$ plan is more discriminating than either of the previous plans.

Our past information about the process quality was based on taking samples of 200 items. If we are now going to use the designed sampling plan, we must take samples of 322. This means that we should use the same number for our p-charts, and new control limits will therefore have to be calculated.

One thing which we must always remember is that the use of an acceptance sampling plan does not, in itself, act as a control over quality. What it does is to provide us with a means of deciding what action to take depending on the current level of process quality.

9-5   COMPARING OC CURVES

If we are to compare sampling plans by means of their OC curves, we must hold some things constant and vary only one factor, if possible. A comparison of Figures 9-2 and 9-3 is such an example. Here n was held constant and c changed from 10 to 6. These two curves, together with a curve for $c = 2$, are shown in Figure 9-5(a), and we can see that as c becomes smaller the curves move progressively to the left and become steeper. The tabulated values for drawing the $n = 200$, $c = 2$ curve are as follows:

Pa	np	p
0.989	0.45	0.0023
0.959	0.75	0.0038
0.945	0.85	0.0043
0.920	1.00	0.0050
0.900	1.10	0.0055
0.809	1.50	0.0075
0.731	1.80	0.0090
0.570	2.40	0.0120
0.340	3.40	0.0170
0.210	4.20	0.0210
0.125	5.00	0.0250
0.095	5.40	0.0270
0.062	6.00	0.0300
0.030	7.00	0.0350
0.019	7.60	0.0380
0.004	9.50	0.0475
0.000	12.50	0.0625

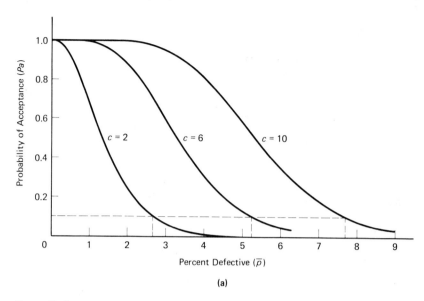

Figure 9-5 (a) Comparison of LTPD Values on OC Curves when $n = 200$; (b) Comparison of AQL Values on OC Curves When $n = 200$; (c) Comparison of Process Means on OC Curves When $n = 200$

With the sample size held constant, the smaller the c value the more discriminating the sample plan. Or, looking at the curves from another point of view, we could say that if we accept a constant consumer's risk of 0.10, the lower the LTPD that we have to meet, the lower the c value will have to be, and the better will be the discriminating ability of the plan. For example, when $n = 200$,

$$c = 10 \text{ when LTPD} = 7.70\%$$
$$c = 6 \text{ when LTPD} = 5.20\%$$
$$c = 2 \text{ when LTPD} = 2.65\%$$

Even if we held AQL constant, a lower LTPD would give a more discriminating plan.

If we now look at Figure 9-5(b) and compare the AQL values at a constant α of 0.05, we see that here also a lower AQL is asso-

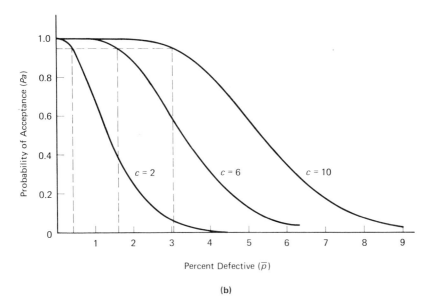

(b)

Figure 9–5 (cont.)

ciated with a lower c value. Summarizing these two characteristics we find, when $n = 200$;

c	LTPD	AQL
10	7.70	3.05
6	5.20	1.60
2	2.65	0.40

From a c of 10 to a c of 2 the LTPD drops by 5.05% and the AQL by 2.65%. Although all three curves move to the left at both the top and the bottom, the bottom does so by a greater absolute amount, thus making the curves steeper and the plans more discriminating.

Another type of comparison can be made by looking at Figure 9-5(c). Here a comparison is made of the probabilities of acceptance at three different levels of average process percent defective: 1, 3, and 5%.

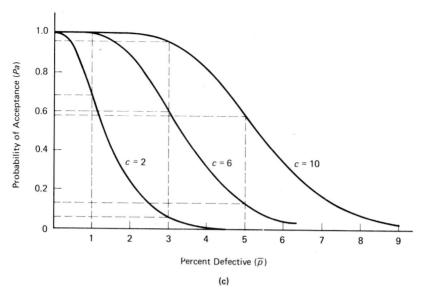

Figure 9–5 (cont.)

Process Average	Probability of Acceptance		
Percent Defective	$c = 2$	$c = 6$	$c = 10$
1	0.68	Close to 1.0	Close to 1.0
3	0.06	0.60	0.96
5	Zero	0.13	0.58

At a process mean of 1% the only plan of the three which will result in any rejections is the $c = 2$ plan; the other two will almost certainly result in 100% acceptance. At a process mean of 3%, all three will result in some acceptance and some rejection, but at $c = 10$ there will be few rejections, and at $c = 2$ there will be few acceptances. At a process mean of 5% the $c = 6$ and the $c = 10$ plans will both result in some acceptance and some rejection, but the $c = 2$ plan will almost certainly result in 100% rejection of the lots.

It is therefore obvious from these three comparisons that, from the producer's point of view, the parameters of a sampling plan must be related to the actual quality conditions existing in the process. Preferably, AQL should be greater than the process mean; otherwise, we would have a condition similar to the accepting of a specification for a variable where this specification is narrower than the process capability. In the latter case, by chance alone, some of the variable values will be beyond the specification, and product will be rejected without any assignable cause being involved.

In the case of the sampling plan where AQL is less than the process mean, inspection costs will be excessive because of the lower probability of accepting at the mean than at the AQL. The producer working with an AQL lower than $\bar{p}$ must either make such process changes as are necessary to improve the quality of his product or negotiate with his customer for a less demanding sampling plan.

If we were now to hold the c value constant at 6 and change the sample size, we could compare the effects of these changes on sampling effectiveness. The following table lists the plotting points for two OC curves where sample sizes are 150 and 300:

Pa	np	p n = 150	p n = 300
0.995	2.0	0.013	0.007
0.976	2.8	0.019	0.009
0.955	3.2	0.021	0.011
0.909	3.8	0.025	0.013
0.791	4.8	0.032	0.016
0.702	5.4	0.036	0.018
0.511	6.6	0.044	0.022
0.450	7.0	0.047	0.023
0.207	9.0	0.060	0.030
0.130	10.0	0.067	0.033
0.079	11.0	0.073	0.037
0.035	12.5	0.083	0.042

These two curves together with the $n = 200$ curve are shown in Figure 9-6, and we can see here that as the sample size increases the plans become more discriminating. For example,

$$\text{LTPD} = 6.9\% \text{ when } n = 150$$

$$\text{LTPD} = 5.2\% \text{ when } n = 200$$

$$\text{LTPD} = 3.5\% \text{ when } n = 300$$

If we are using acceptance sampling and we want to tighten up our inspection, we may either increase the size of the sample or decrease the acceptance number. Whichever method we adopt, we should redraw the OC curve so as to compare the new acceptance levels with those of the original plan.

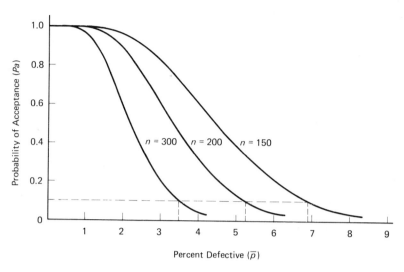

Figure 9–6 Comparison of OC Curves When $c = 6$

9-6 OUTGOING QUALITY

The very use of an acceptance sampling plan will improve the level of quality of the product being shipped to the customer, that is, if no inspection plan had been used before. The reason for this is that all defectives found in the samples will be removed and either corrected or replaced by good product. So, even if all lots were at an acceptable level, the quality would be improved by the removal of defectives from the samples.

If a sampling plan has been properly designed for a particular process, the OC curve should cover a range of percent defective over which there is **some** probability of the actual results occurring. For example, at AQL there is a 0.95 probability of acceptance, so that, **in the long run,** when $\bar{p} = $ AQL, 95 batches out of 100 will be accepted and 5 will be rejected. Because the rejected lots will be corrected, the *average outgoing quality* (AOQ) will not be AQL, but AQL times its probability of acceptance, and the same will be true for any value of p.

Using the $n = 322$, $c = 11$ plan as as example, at AQL,

$$AOQ = 0.95 \times 0.0215$$

$$= 0.0204$$

Ninety five batches out of 100 will be accepted as is, and 5 will be corrected (and have no defectives), so the outgoing quality will be 2.04% defective when the process is running at 2.15% defective.

Similarly, at LTPD,

$$AOQ = 0.10 \times 0.00523$$

$$= 0.0052$$

Here only 10 lots in 100 will be accepted when the process is running at 5.23% defective, and the remaining 90 will have to be corrected, resulting in an outgoing quality level of only 0.52% defective. This is an extreme drop in the level of defectives, but it must not be mistaken for a desirable condition. The costs of finding (inspection) and replacing (or repairing) the defectives make it extremely uneconomical to operate at the LTPD level. In fact, under those conditions many operators would revert to 100% inspection until the process average is brought back into line.

These calculations for AOQ can be carried out for all the points used to construct our OC curves and new curves drawn which represent the change in outgoing quality with change in process percent defective. The coordinates for plotting the AOQ curves for the three $c = 6$ plans are tabulated as follows:

	$n = 150$		$n = 200$		$n = 300$	
Pa	p	AOQ (pPa)	p	AOQ (pPa)	p	AOQ (pPa)
0.995	0.013	0.0129	0.010	0.010	0.007	0.0070
0.976	0.019	0.0185	0.014	0.0137	0.009	0.0088
0.955	0.021	0.0201	0.016	0.0153	0.011	0.0105
0.909	0.025	0.0227	0.019	0.0173	0.013	0.0118
0.791	0.032	0.0253	0.024	0.0190	0.016	0.0127
0.702	0.036	0.0253	0.027	0.0190	0.018	0.0126
0.511	0.044	0.0225	0.033	0.0169	0.022	0.0112
0.450	0.047	0.0212	0.035	0.0158	0.023	0.0104
0.207	0.060	0.0124	0.045	0.0093	0.030	0.0062
0.130	0.067	0.0087	0.050	0.0065	0.033	0.0043

Figure 9-7 shows the AOQ curves for each of these plans, and the first characteristic which we should note is that each rises to a maximum and then drops off again. This maximum value is known

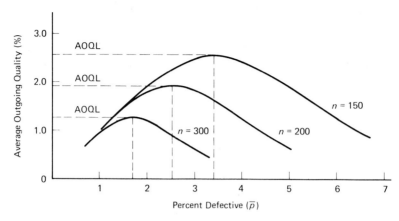

Figure 9–7   Comparison of AOQ Curves When c = 6

as the *average outgoing quality limit* (AOQL) and is the highest **average** outgoing level of defectives associated with a particular plan.

Figure 9-7 provides the following information about the three plans:

When n = 150 and $\bar{p}$ = 3.4%,   AOQL = 2.6%

When n = 200 and $\bar{p}$ = 2.5%,   AOQL = 1.9%

When n = 300 and $\bar{p}$ = 1.7%,   AOQL = 1.3%

This comparison tells us that as the OC curves move to the left so do the AOQ curves, and as the sample size increases (with constant c) the percentage of defectives being shipped out to the customer decreases. So we now have another means of comparing plans, and the AOQ curve should generally be drawn at the same time as the OC curve.

It is important to emphasize that, while we may compare plans on the basis of their average outgoing quality limits, we must never lose sight of the fact that the key word here is "average." It is not an **absolute** maximum that it represents but an **average** maximum, and, as an average is a measure of central tendency, some will be above and some below this level. In some ways it can be compared to saying that the **average** percentage of heads obtained when a coin is tossed ten times will be 50%, but we are all quite well aware of the fact that in most cases the result will be either above or below this level. Once again our attention is drawn to the fact that carrying out a calculation on a probability does not convert it into a certainty; it is still a probability, perhaps a high one, but still a probability.

Nevertheless, the determination of AOQL does provide an objective means of comparing plans, especially when both the sample size and the acceptance numbers differ or when the OC curves appear to be similar.

9-7   OTHER SAMPLING PLANS

The taking of large samples can be costly, so *Normal*, *Tightened*, and *Reduced* inspection plans have been devised which allow for a reduction in inspection when a process is operating satisfactorily relative to the specified AQL. If a specified number of lots have been accepted under Normal inspection, the plans allow for a smaller Reduced n and c number to be used. Then, if successive lots are rejected, inspection reverts to Normal, and, with further rejections, to Tightened inspection with an even smaller acceptance number. There are obvious cost advantages here for the well-run plant when, for example, it may be possible to drop from a sample size of 200 to one of only 80.

In addition, double and multiple sampling plans may bring about further reductions in inspection costs. A double sampling plan, for example, might call for a first sample of 80 items with an acceptance value of three and a rejection value of seven. That is,

$$n_1 = 80, \qquad c_1 = 3, \qquad c_2 = 7$$

Under this plan we would accept the lot if the first sample contained three or less defectives, we would reject it if there were seven or more defectives, but we would draw a second sample of 80 if there were four, five, or six defectives. At the next stage we may have

$$n_2 = 160, \qquad c_3 = 8, \qquad c_4 = 9$$

where n_2 is the cumulative sample.

We would now accept the lot if the total of all defectives in both samples did not exceed eight and we would reject the lot if there were nine or more. Multiple sampling plans follow the same type of patterns but have a greater number of steps and hence an opportunity to start with an even smaller sample size.

When customers desire to have their suppliers' inspection plans conform to an accepted standard, they may wish to specify a plan from the U.S. Military Standard 105D or International Standard ISO/DIS–2859. These standards contain predesigned single, double, and multiple sampling plans, and the reader who desires more information on this subject should consult one of these published standards.

QUESTIONS AND PROBLEMS

---

1. What is meant by the acceptance number of a sampling plan?

2. What criterion is generally used to determine whether to scrap or rework a defective item?

3. Draw an "ideal" OC curve to represent the situation when the acceptable quality level is 2.5%.

4. (a) Describe what is meant by "acceptable quality level."
   (b) Describe what is meant by "lot tolerance percent defective."

5. (a) Describe the "consumer's risk."
   (b) Describe the "producer's risk."

6. By interpolating in the Poisson cumulative table, find the np value when the probability of accepting four or less is 0.900.

7. Draw the OC curve for the plan $n = 200$, $c = 4$.

8. What is meant when we say that one plan is more "discriminating" than another?

9. By means of OC curves, compare the plans $n = 400$, $c = 12$; and $n = 100$, $c = 3$.

10. (a) What effect does c have on the discriminating power of a sampling plan?
    (b) What effect does n have on the discriminating power of a sampling plan?

11. (a) Describe what is meant by "average outgoing quality."
    (b) Describe what is meant by "average outgoing quality limit."

12. If the AOQ is 2.0% when a process is running at its AQL and 0.5% when it is running at its LTPD, should the operators at-

tempt to have the process run at its LTPD? Explain the reason for your answer.

13. Draw the AOQ curves for the sampling plans described in question 9, and state your conclusions from examining these curves.

14. What is the purpose in using a double or multiple sampling plan?

10

Other Aspects of Quality Control

10-1   STATISTICAL ANALYSIS

The adoption of the procedures outlined in the preceding chapters will usually bring about a start to the leveling out of fluctuations in product and process variables and in numbers of defects and defectives. Even the indirect "cop-on-the-beat" effect can produce results before any deliberate corrective action is taken. It is often surprising how much better results can be when an operator becomes aware of the fact that someone is not only interested in, but is carefully watching the outcome of, his or her efforts.

The adoption of quality-control procedures will make it possible to identify abnormal variations caused by some specific event or condition and avoid wasting time looking for causes when the variations are normal. The means $\bar{x}$, $\bar{p}$, $\bar{c}$, and $\bar{u}$ can be watched closely and long-term shifts can be avoided where these are in the direction of loss of technical control.

However, there may be other information which could be obtained from the quality-control data which will require further study of the subject. For example, a breakdown by production center may reveal that two or more centers have different means. These differ-

209

ences could occur by chance alone, or they could be due to the fact that more than one universe of values exists. If they are due to chance, then attempting to make adjustments might only result in further confusion. The techniques for checking the statistical significance of differences in means is beyond the scope of this text, and the interested reader is advised to consult one of the more advanced statistical works.

Also, there is the problem of assigning a significance to a *run*. A run exists when a number of values are all on one side of the mean or are all in either an increasing or a decreasing series. These things also happen by chance alone, or they may be due to changes in the process. Statistical techniques exist which enable a statement to be made about the level of significance of a run, but these also are beyond the scope of this text.

It is the decision about which quality characteristics to study and the establishment of $\bar{x} - R$, p, c, or u charts which bring about the first major step in the direction of increased control. All the other aspects are refinements which can follow at a later date.

10-2   SPECIAL APPLICATIONS

It has already been shown that quality-control techniques can be used in the study of accident frequency, but there are other areas of management where they can also be used to advantage. As we have seen, attributes are either one thing or another, they have no in-between values, and attribute controls are therefore appropriate for management-by-exception applications. For example, a work order may be behind schedule, on schedule, or ahead of schedule; there are no other possibilities. The one which we are most interested in is the condition of being behind schedule, and we can say that an order is either behind schedule or it is not. The binomial distribution is therefore appropriate, and p-charts could be used to measure the effectiveness of production control procedures.

Similarly, a person is either at work or not at work, and $\bar{p}$-charts may be of use to the personnel department to keep track of absenteeism. Such charting may reveal cyclical trends or assignable causes under specific conditions of labor-management relations. It may also show up a gradual trend and enable corrective measures to be taken with some source of discontent before conditions become out of control and result in a work stoppage.

There are obviously many potential applications for quality-control techniques in areas other than manufacturing, and the same cost rules apply. They should only be used where the cost advantage, or potential advantage, exceeds the cost of the control procedures.

10-3   QUALITY ASSURANCE

Statistical quality-control procedures are tools which are used to ensure that processes operate consistently within their capabilities and that products leave the plant at acceptable levels of quality. They are indeed important tools, but tools nevertheless, among a number of others. These quality-control tools enable nontechnical personnel to give invaluable assistance to those in charge of the technical processes, and where they are carried out by the latter, they become an integral part of the overall process control.

After all this emphasis on its importance and on the need for further study, it may come as a surprise to learn that statistical quality control is just one aspect of a much larger subject, quality assurance. To some it may be the single most important aspect, especially where repetitive manufacturing is involved, but to others it may take its place behind technology and alongside documentation and other procedural controls.

Quality assurance is the whole business of arranging for **all** the necessary prerequisites to the production of a satisfactory product. Where the product is a one-of-a-kind high-technology assembly, documentation and certification at various stages in the operation can be just as important as $\bar{x} - R$ charts are to a continuous process. Where the appropriate precautions are assured, the customer can feel confident that the purchased item will be what was ordered and will perform as was intended.

Suppose that some internal component in a centrifugal pump were made of a sub-standard material; it could not be seen after assembly was completed, and the pump might quite likely pass all required running tests. It might be some months or even years before the component would fail, but if this happened suddenly, the pump could be ruined and whatever it serviced could be shut down. Perhaps there would be no water to fight a fire, or a boiler would be ruined, or an electric generator would be shut down. In any of these events the resultant costs could be considerable, and it would therefore make good sense to tolerate a slightly higher initial cost in order to be assured that the correct quality was there in the first place.

To prevent this type of occurrence, we might institute a set of procedures to (1) check that the specification on the raw-material purchase order agrees with that on the engineering drawing; (2) have the supplier certify that the materials shipped are to the correct specification; (3) have incoming inspection send test pieces to a laboratory for verification of the specification; (4) check that the correct material is issued from the raw-material stores; (5) ensure that, if any off-specification material is found, it will be suitably identified and disposed of.

With some processes it is not always possible to provide a high enough level of assurance by inspection. It is then necessary to have operators certified as to level of competence, written operating procedures which must be followed to the letter, and perhaps some type of certification that the procedures were actually carried out. For example, only certain specified personnel may be permitted to operate a heat-treatment furnace; the heating, soaking, and cooling times may be specified; and a chart from the temperature recorder may have to be certified by a competent person.

There are obviously a great many aspects to quality assurance and the potential for an almost limitless number of levels of assurance. The level of assurance that we would want would depend, for example, on the level of technology involved, the complexity of an assembly, the location of the part in the assembly, and the risks to human health and safety that might result from the failure of a part. So a quality assurance program might be comprised, simply, of an organization chart stating who does what in the process, the keeping of quality records, and the calibration of testing or measuring equipment. On the other hand, it might start right at the beginning with formal provisions for design verification, written procedures for all stages in processing and inspection, purchase order verification, supplier rating, qualifications of special-process personnel, control and disposition of all quality documents, disposition of nonconforming items and material, types of permissible corrective action, and many other factors too numerous to mention.

The business of selecting the level of quality assurance that is appropriate has been simplified by the development of a number of national standards. A customer can determine what level is required and then specify that level in the purchase order or contract, and the manufacturer must then meet the requirements of that particular published standard. Some examples of quality assurance standards are the following:

AMERICAN

ASQC C-1   General requirements for a quality program

ANSI N45.2   Quality assurance program requirements for nuclear power plants

MIL-1-45208   Inspection system requirements

MIL-Q-9858A   Quality program requirements

10CFR50 Appendix B   Quality assurance criteria for nuclear power plants and fuel reprocessing plants

BRITISH

BS 5179 Part 1   Final inspection system

BS 5179 Part 2   Comprehensive inspection system

BS 5179 Part 3   Comprehensive quality control system

CANADIAN

Z299.1   Quality assurance program requirements

Z299.2   Quality control program requirements

Z299.3   Quality verification program requirements

Z299.4   Inspection program requirements

DND 1015   Quality program requirements for contractors

DND 1016   Contractor's inspection system requirements

DND 1017   Basic inspection requirements for contractors

10-4   RECOMMENDED READING

It was stated in the Preface that the purpose of this book was to provide a basis for the initial establishment of control procedures and that advanced theory would be avoided. Now that the reading has been completed and presumably a start made to some type of systematic rational controls, it may not be long before a need is felt for additional information.

The library at a local university or college would be an ideal place to find more advanced material, but in case this is not convenient, the following list may be of some assistance. It must not be thought of as being a complete list, and no slight is intended to any author who has been omitted. It is simply a collection of books which the author has enjoyed reading and which he would like to recommend to others.

BESTERFIELD, DALE H., *Quality Control*. Englewood Cliffs, N.J.: Prentice-Hall, Inc., 1979.

CHARBONNEAU, HARVEY C., AND GORDON L. WEBSTER, *Industrial Quality Control*. Englewood Cliffs, N.J.: Prentice-Hall, Inc., 1978.

DUNCAN, ACHESON J., *Quality Control and Industrial Statistics* (4th ed.) Homewood, Ill.: Richard D. Irwin, Inc., 1974.

FEIGENBAUM, A. V., *Total Quality Control: Engineering and Management*. New York: McGraw-Hill Book Co., 1961.

GRANT, EUGENE L., and RICHARD S. LEAVENWORTH, *Statistical Quality Control*. New York: McGraw-Hill Book Co., 1974.

HALPERN, SIGMUND, *The Assurance Sciences: An Introduction to Quality Control and Reliability*. Englewood Cliffs, N.J.: Prentice-Hall, Inc., 1978.

HANSEN, BERTRAND L., *Quality Control: Theory and Applications*. Englewood Cliffs, N.J.: Prentice-Hall, Inc., 1963.

OTT, ELLIS R., *Process Quality Control*. New York: McGraw-Hill Book Co., 1975.

Good luck and success in your endeavors.

Appendixes

APPENDIX 1   *Areas and Ordinates of the Normal Curve*

TABLE OF AREAS AND ORDINATES OF THE NORMAL CURVE*

z	Area Under the Curve Between μ and x	Ordinate (Y) (Frequency)	z	Area Under the Curve Between μ and x	Ordinate (Y) (Frequency)
0.00	0.00000	0.39894	0.35	0.13683	0.37524
0.01	0.00399	0.39892	0.36	0.14058	0.37391
0.02	0.00798	0.39886	0.37	0.14431	0.37255
0.03	0.01197	0.39876	0.38	0.14803	0.37115
0.04	0.01595	0.39862	0.39	0.15173	0.36973
0.05	0.01994	0.39844	0.40	0.15542	0.36827
0.06	0.02392	0.39822	0.41	0.15910	0.36678
0.07	0.02790	0.39797	0.42	0.16276	0.36526
0.08	0.03188	0.39767	0.43	0.16640	0.36371
0.09	0.03586	0.39733	0.44	0.17003	0.36213
0.10	0.03983	0.39695	0.45	0.17364	0.36053
0.11	0.04380	0.39654	0.46	0.17724	0.35889
0.12	0.04776	0.39608	0.47	0.18082	0.35723
0.13	0.05172	0.39559	0.48	0.18439	0.35553
0.14	0.05567	0.39505	0.49	0.18793	0.35381
0.15	0.05962	0.39448	0.50	0.19146	0.35207
0.16	0.06356	0.39387	0.51	0.19497	0.35029
0.17	0.06749	0.39322	0.52	0.19847	0.34849
0.18	0.07142	0.39253	0.53	0.20194	0.34667
0.19	0.07535	0.39181	0.54	0.20540	0.34482
0.20	0.07926	0.39104	0.55	0.20884	0.34294
0.21	0.08317	0.39024	0.56	0.21226	0.34105
0.22	0.08706	0.38940	0.57	0.21566	0.33912
0.23	0.09095	0.38853	0.58	0.21904	0.33718
0.24	0.09483	0.38762	0.59	0.22240	0.33521
0.25	0.09871	0.38667	0.60	0.22575	0.33322
0.26	0.10257	0.38568	0.61	0.22907	0.33121
0.27	0.10642	0.38466	0.62	0.23237	0.32918
0.28	0.11026	0.38361	0.63	0.23565	0.32713
0.29	0.11409	0.38251	0.64	0.23891	0.32506
0.30	0.11791	0.38139	0.65	0.24215	0.32297
0.31	0.12172	0.38023	0.66	0.24537	0.32086
0.32	0.12552	0.37903	0.67	0.24857	0.31874
0.33	0.12930	0.37780	0.68	0.25175	0.31659
0.34	0.13307	0.37654	0.69	0.25490	0.31443

(a)

TABLE OF AREAS AND ORDINATES OF THE NORMAL CURVE* (cont.)

z	Area Under the Curve Between μ and x	Ordinate (Y) (Frequency)	z	Area Under the Curve Between μ and x	Ordinate (Y) (Frequency)
0.70	0.25804	0.31225	1.10	0.36433	0.21785
0.71	0.26115	0.31006	1.11	0.36650	0.21546
0.72	0.26424	0.30785	1.12	0.36864	0.21307
0.73	0.26730	0.30563	1.13	0.37076	0.21069
0.74	0.27035	0.30339	1.14	0.37286	0.20831
0.75	0.27337	0.30114	1.15	0.37493	0.20594
0.76	0.27637	0.29887	1.16	0.37698	0.20357
0.77	0.27935	0.29659	1.17	0.37900	0.20121
0.78	0.28230	0.29431	1.18	0.38100	0.19886
0.79	0.28524	0.29200	1.19	0.38298	0.19652
0.80	0.28814	0.28969	1.20	0.38493	0.19419
0.81	0.29103	0.28737	1.21	0.38686	0.19186
0.82	0.29389	0.28504	1.22	0.38877	0.18954
0.83	0.29673	0.28269	1.23	0.39065	0.18724
0.84	0.29955	0.28034	1.24	0.39251	0.18494
0.85	0.30234	0.27798	1.25	0.39435	0.18265
0.86	0.30511	0.27562	1.26	0.39617	0.18037
0.87	0.30785	0.27324	1.27	0.39796	0.17810
0.88	0.31057	0.27086	1.28	0.39973	0.17585
0.89	0.31327	0.26848	1.29	0.40147	0.17360
0.90	0.31594	0.26609	1.30	0.40320	0.17137
0.91	0.31859	0.26369	1.31	0.40490	0.16915
0.92	0.32121	0.26129	1.32	0.40658	0.16694
0.93	0.32381	0.25888	1.33	0.40824	0.16474
0.94	0.32639	0.25647	1.34	0.40988	0.16256
0.95	0.32894	0.25406	1.35	0.41149	0.16038
0.96	0.33147	0.25164	1.36	0.41309	0.15822
0.97	0.33398	0.24923	1.37	0.41466	0.15608
0.98	0.33646	0.24681	1.38	0.41621	0.15395
0.99	0.33891	0.24439	1.39	0.41774	0.15183
1.00	0.34134	0.24197	1.40	0.41924	0.14973
1.01	0.34375	0.23955	1.41	0.42073	0.14764
1.02	0.34614	0.23713	1.42	0.42220	0.14556
1.03	0.34850	0.23471	1.43	0.42364	0.14350
1.04	0.35083	0.23230	1.44	0.42507	0.14146
1.05	0.35314	0.22988	1.45	0.42647	0.13943
1.06	0.35543	0.22747	1.46	0.42786	0.13742
1.07	0.35769	0.22506	1.47	0.42922	0.13542
1.08	0.35993	0.22265	1.48	0.43056	0.13344
1.09	0.36214	0.22025	1.49	0.43189	0.13147

(b)

z	Area Under the Curve Between μ and x	Ordinate (Y) (Frequency)	z	Area Under the Curve Between μ and x	Ordinate (Y) (Frequency)
1.50	0.43319	0.12952	1.90	0.47128	0.06562
1.51	0.43448	0.12758	1.91	0.47193	0.06438
1.52	0.43574	0.12566	1.92	0.47257	0.06316
1.53	0.43699	0.12376	1.93	0.47320	0.06195
1.54	0.43822	0.12188	1.94	0.47381	0.06077
1.55	0.43943	0.12001	1.95	0.47441	0.05959
1.56	0.44062	0.11816	1.96	0.47500	0.05844
1.57	0.44179	0.11632	1.97	0.47558	0.05730
1.58	0.44295	0.11450	1.98	0.47615	0.05618
1.59	0.44408	0.11270	1.99	0.47670	0.05508
1.60	0.44520	0.11092	2.00	0.47725	0.05399
1.61	0.44630	0.10915	2.01	0.47778	0.05292
1.62	0.44738	0.10741	2.02	0.47831	0.05186
1.63	0.44845	0.10567	2.03	0.47882	0.05082
1.64	0.44950	0.10396	2.04	0.47932	0.04980
1.65	0.45053	0.10226	2.05	0.47982	0.04879
1.66	0.45154	0.10059	2.06	0.48030	0.04780
1.67	0.45254	0.09893	2.07	0.48077	0.04682
1.68	0.45352	0.09728	2.08	0.48124	0.04586
1.69	0.45449	0.09566	2.09	0.48169	0.04491
1.70	0.45543	0.09405	2.10	0.48214	0.04398
1.71	0.45637	0.09246	2.11	0.48257	0.04307
1.72	0.45728	0.09089	2.12	0.48300	0.04217
1.73	0.45818	0.08933	2.13	0.48341	0.04128
1.74	0.45907	0.08780	2.14	0.48382	0.04041
1.75	0.45994	0.08628	2.15	0.48422	0.03955
1.76	0.46080	0.08478	2.16	0.48461	0.03871
1.77	0.46164	0.08329	2.17	0.48500	0.03788
1.78	0.46246	0.08183	2.18	0.48537	0.03706
1.79	0.46327	0.08038	2.19	0.48574	0.03626
1.80	0.46407	0.07895	2.20	0.48610	0.03547
1.81	0.46485	0.07754	2.21	0.48645	0.03470
1.82	0.46562	0.07614	2.22	0.48679	0.03394
1.83	0.46638	0.07477	2.23	0.48713	0.03319
1.84	0.46712	0.07341	2.24	0.48745	0.03246
1.85	0.46784	0.07206	2.25	0.48778	0.03174
1.86	0.46856	0.07074	2.26	0.48809	0.03103
1.87	0.46926	0.06943	2.27	0.48840	0.03034
1.88	0.46995	0.06814	2.28	0.48870	0.02965
1.39	0.47062	0.06687	2.29	0.48899	0.02898

(c)

z	Area Under the Curve Between μ and x	Ordinate (Y) (Frequency)	z	Area Under the Curve Between μ and x	Ordinate (Y) (Frequency)
2.30	0.48928	0.02833	2.70	0.49653	0.01042
2.31	0.48956	0.02768	2.71	0.49664	0.01014
2.32	0.48983	0.02705	2.72	0.49674	0.00987
2.33	0.49010	0.02643	2.73	0.49683	0.00961
2.34	0.49036	0.02582	2.74	0.49693	0.00935
2.35	0.49064	0.02522	2.75	0.49702	0.00909
2.36	0.49086	0.02463	2.76	0.49711	0.00885
2.37	0.49111	0.02406	2.77	0.49720	0.00861
2.38	0.49134	0.02349	2.78	0.49728	0.00837
2.39	0.49158	0.02294	2.79	0.49736	0.00814
2.40	0.49180	0.02239	2.80	0.49744	0.00792
2.41	0.49202	0.02186	2.81	0.49752	0.00770
2.42	0.49224	0.02134	2.82	0.49760	0.00748
2.43	0.49245	0.02083	2.83	0.49767	0.00727
2.44	0.49266	0.02033	2.84	0.49774	0.00707
2.45	0.49286	0.01984	2.85	0.49781	0.00687
2.46	0.49305	0.01936	2.86	0.49788	0.00668
2.47	0.49324	0.01889	2.87	0.49795	0.00649
2.48	0.49343	0.01842	2.88	0.49801	0.00631
2.49	0.49361	0.01797	2.89	0.49807	0.00613
2.50	0.49379	0.01753	2.90	0.49813	0.00595
2.51	0.49396	0.01709	2.91	0.49819	0.00578
2.52	0.49413	0.01667	2.92	0.49825	0.00562
2.53	0.49430	0.01625	2.93	0.49831	0.00545
2.54	0.49446	0.01585	2.94	0.49836	0.00530
2.55	0.49461	0.01545	2.95	0.49841	0.00514
2.56	0.49477	0.01506	2.96	0.49846	0.00499
2.57	0.49492	0.01468	2.97	0.49851	0.00485
2.58	0.49506	0.01431	2.98	0.49856	0.00471
2.59	0.49520	0.01394	2.99	0.49861	0.00457
2.60	0.49534	0.01358	3.00	0.49865	0.00443
2.61	0.49547	0.01323	3.01	0.49869	0.00430
2.62	0.49560	0.01289	3.02	0.49874	0.00417
2.63	0.49573	0.01256	3.03	0.49878	0.00405
2.64	0.49585	0.01223	3.04	0.49882	0.00393
2.65	0.49598	0.01191	3.05	0.49886	0.00381
2.66	0.49609	0.01160	3.06	0.49889	0.00370
2.67	0.49621	0.01130	3.07	0.49893	0.00358
2.68	0.49632	0.01100	3.08	0.49897	0.00348
2.69	0.49643	0.01071	3.09	0.49900	0.00337

(d)

z	Area Under the Curve Between μ and x	Ordinate (Y) (Frequency)	z	Area Under the Curve Between μ and x	Ordinate (Y) (Frequency)
3.10	0.49903	0.00327	3.50	0.49977	0.00087
3.11	0.49906	0.00317	3.51	0.49978	0.00084
3.12	0.49910	0.00307	3.52	0.49978	0.00081
3.13	0.49913	0.00298	3.53	0.49979	0.00079
3.14	0.49916	0.00288	3.54	0.49980	0.00076
3.15	0.49918	0.00279	3.55	0.49981	0.00073
3.16	0.49921	0.00271	3.56	0.49981	0.00071
3.17	0.49924	0.00262	3.57	0.49982	0.00068
3.18	0.49926	0.00254	3.58	0.49983	0.00066
3.19	0.49929	0.00246	3.59	0.49983	0.00063
3.20	0.49931	0.00238	3.60	0.49984	0.00061
3.21	0.49934	0.00231	3.61	0.49985	0.00059
3.22	0.49936	0.00224	3.62	0.49985	0.00057
3.23	0.49938	0.00216	3.63	0.49986	0.00055
3.24	0.49940	0.00210	3.64	0.49986	0.00053
3.25	0.49942	0.00203	3.65	0.49987	0.00051
3.26	0.49944	0.00196	3.66	0.49987	0.00049
3.27	0.49946	0.00190	3.67	0.49988	0.00047
3.28	0.49948	0.00184	3.68	0.49988	0.00046
3.29	0.49950	0.00178	3.69	0.49989	0.00044
3.30	0.49952	0.00172	3.70	0.49989	0.00042
3.31	0.49953	0.00167	3.71	0.49990	0.00041
3.32	0.49955	0.00161	3.72	0.49990	0.00039
3.33	0.49957	0.00156	3.73	0.49990	0.00038
3.34	0.49958	0.00151	3.74	0.49991	0.00037
3.35	0.49960	0.00146	3.75	0.49991	0.00035
3.36	0.49961	0.00141	3.76	0.49992	0.00034
3.37	0.49962	0.00136	3.77	0.49992	0.00033
3.38	0.49964	0.00132	3.78	0.49992	0.00031
3.39	0.49965	0.00127	3.79	0.49992	0.00030
3.40	0.49966	0.00123	3.80	0.49993	0.00029
3.41	0.49968	0.00119	3.81	0.49993	0.00028
3.42	0.49969	0.00115	3.82	0.49993	0.00027
3.43	0.49970	0.00111	3.83	0.49994	0.00026
3.44	0.49971	0.00107	3.84	0.49994	0.00025
3.45	0.49972	0.00104	3.85	0.49994	0.00024
3.46	0.49973	0.00100	3.86	0.49994	0.00023
3.47	0.49974	0.00097	3.87	0.49995	0.00022
3.48	0.49975	0.00094	3.88	0.49995	0.00021
3.49	0.49976	0.00090	3.89	0.49995	0.00021

(e)

TABLE OF AREAS AND ORDINATES OF THE NORMAL CURVE* (cont.)

z	Area Under the Curve Between μ and x	Ordinate (Y) (Frequency)	z	Area Under the Curve Between μ and x	Ordinate (Y) (Frequency)
3.90	0.49995	0.00020	3.95	0.49996	0.00016
3.91	0.49995	0.00019	3.96	0.49996	0.00016
3.92	0.49996	0.00018	3.97	0.49996	0.00015
3.93	0.49996	0.00018	3.98	0.49997	0.00014
3.94	0.49996	0.00017	3.99	0.49997	0.00014

[a]From J. F. Kenny and G. S. Keeping, *Mathematics of Statistics*. © 1954 by Litton Educational Publishing Inc. Reprinted by permission of D. Van Nostrand Company.

APPENDIX 2   *Random Times*

RANDOM TIMES TABLE
(Minutes after Starting Time)

1	2	3	4	5
0.26	0.54	0.15	0.30	0.35
0.54	0.50	0.54	0.09	0.42
0.42	0.11	0.59	0.45	0.29
0.22	0.51	0.26	0.37	0.12
0.17	0.55	0.31	0.33	0.57
0.58	0.07	0.37	0.11	0.27
0.14	0.53	0.50	0.05	0.55
0.41	0.36	0.35	1.00	0.48
0.04	0.12	0.28	0.02	0.26
0.16	0.17	0.04	0.35	0.30
0.07	0.22	0.10	0.04	0.01
0.49	0.37	0.09	0.18	0.03

6	7	8	9	10
0.41	0.06	0.11	0.37	0.31
0.08	1.00	0.10	0.44	0.37
0.50	0.55	0.17	0.17	0.39
0.49	0.14	0.56	0.41	0.07
0.11	0.35	0.59	0.29	0.41
0.23	0.46	0.08	0.53	0.46
0.03	0.15	0.39	1.00	0.47
0.21	0.28	0.31	0.47	0.44
0.13	0.04	0.36	0.14	0.42
0.14	0.03	0.07	0.26	0.03
0.55	0.34	0.03	0.32	0.30
1.00	0.32	0.42	0.13	0.55

APPENDIX 3 *Sequential Random Times*

SEQUENTIAL RANDOM TIMES TABLE
(Minutes after Starting Time)

1	2	3	4	5
0.04	0.07	0.04	0.02	0.01
0.07	0.11	0.09	0.04	0.03
0.14	0.12	0.10	0.05	0.12
0.16	0.17	0.15	0.09	0.26
0.17	0.22	0.26	0.11	0.27
0.22	0.36	0.28	0.18	0.29
0.26	0.37	0.31	0.30	0.30
0.41	0.50	0.35	0.33	0.35
0.42	0.51	0.37	0.35	0.42
0.49	0.53	0.50	0.37	0.48
0.54	0.54	0.54	0.45	0.55
0.58	0.55	0.59	1.00	0.57

6	7	8	9	10
0.02	0.03	0.03	0.13	0.03
0.03	0.04	0.07	0.14	0.07
0.08	0.06	0.08	0.17	0.30
0.11	0.14	0.10	0.26	0.31
0.13	0.15	0.11	0.29	0.37
0.14	0.28	0.17	0.32	0.39
0.23	0.32	0.31	0.37	0.41
0.41	0.34	0.36	0.41	0.42
0.49	0.35	0.39	0.44	0.44
0.50	0.46	0.42	0.47	0.46
0.55	0.55	0.56	0.53	0.47
1.00	1.00	0.59	1.00	0.55

RANDOM NUMBERS

1	2	3	4
2680	5365	1994	4218
8742	5730	3274	8072
2406	0358	5899	2917
4171	4511	8455	9524
1922	6441	0074	6495
7014	8222	0088	7976
7051	3179	1187	1080
0180	8830	0135	5395
4604	0488	3103	0025
3465	0061	9596	8946
8125	2075	2754	3600
1460	8024	6824	7861
7230	1998	9355	2736
4736	7459	4841	0319
2498	1541	2469	1845
0018	1742	2178	3132
0023	2340	8578	2560
6971	6628	9435	8618
0198	6381	8261	6869
1229	9632	5845	0085
2219	6003	0087	0006
9331	7215	0001	3987
9501	7648	6150	3180
5685	4469	4621	3479
8857	4357	0598	0683

APPENDIX 5   *Factors for Control Charts*

FACTORS FOR CONTROL CHARTS

Sample Size n	Factor for: Average A_2	Factor for: Range D_3	Factor for: Range D_4
2	1.880	0.0	3.268
3	1.023	0.0	2.574
4	0.729	0.0	2.282
5	0.577	0.0	2.114
6	0.483	0.0	2.004
7	0.419	0.076	1.924
8	0.373	0.136	1.864
9	0.337	0.184	1.816
10	0.308	0.223	1.777
11	0.285	0.256	1.744
12	0.266	0.284	1.717
13	0.249	0.308	1.692
14	0.235	0.329	1.671
15	0.223	0.348	1.652

Formulas for computing control limits:

$$UCL_{\bar{x}} = \bar{\bar{x}} + A_2\bar{R}$$

$$LCL_{\bar{x}} = \bar{\bar{x}} - A_2\bar{R}$$

$$UCL_R = D_4\bar{R}$$

$$LCL_R = D_3\bar{R}$$

For the benefit of those who are conversant with regression analysis, the coefficient of determination (r^2) is 0.9965 and the correlation coefficient (r) 0.9983. These give a student's t test value of 29.23, indicating that this correlation is statistically highly significant. It must be remembered, of course, that the equation shown in Figure 6-1 applies only to the particular variable in our example. Any other variable would have its own specific constant values.

APPENDIX 7 *Selected Values of the Poisson Cumulative Distribution*

SELECTED VALUES OF THE POISSON CUMULATIVE DISTRIBUTION[a]
(Probability of c or less occurrences)

c or r	0.02	0.04	0.06	0.08	0.10	0.15	0.20	0.25	0.30	0.35	0.40	0.45	0.50	0.55	0.60
											μ or np				
0	0.980	0.961	0.912	0.923	0.905	0.861	0.819	0.779	0.741	0.705	0.670	0.638	0.607	0.577	0.549
1	1.000	0.999	0.998	0.977	0.995	0.990	0.982	0.974	0.963	0.951	0.938	0.925	0.910	0.894	0.878
2		1.000	1.000	1.000	1.000	0.999	0.999	0.998	0.996	0.994	0.992	0.989	0.986	0.982	0.977
3						1.000	1.000	1.000	1.000	1.000	0.999	0.999	0.998	0.998	0.997
4											1.000	1.000	1.000	1.000	1.000

c or r	0.65	0.70	0.75	0.80	0.85	0.90	0.95	1.00	1.1	1.2	1.3	1.4	1.5	1.6	1.7
											μ or np				
0	0.522	0.497	0.472	0.449	0.427	0.407	0.387	0.368	0.333	0.301	0.273	0.247	0.223	0.202	0.183
1	0.861	0.844	0.827	0.809	0.791	0.772	0.754	0.736	0.699	0.663	0.627	0.592	0.558	0.525	0.493
2	0.972	0.966	0.959	0.953	0.945	0.937	0.929	0.920	0.900	0.879	0.857	0.833	0.809	0.783	0.757
3	0.996	0.994	0.993	0.991	0.989	0.987	0.984	0.981	0.974	0.966	0.957	0.946	0.934	0.921	0.907
4	0.999	0.999	0.999	0.999	0.998	0.998	0.997	0.996	0.995	0.992	0.989	0.986	0.981	0.976	0.970
5	1.000	1.000	1.000	1.000	1.000	1.000	1.000	0.999	0.999	0.998	0.998	0.997	0.996	0.994	0.992
6								1.000	1.000	1.000	1.000	0.999	0.999	0.999	0.998
7												1.000	1.000	1.000	1.000

c or r	1.8	1.9	2.0	2.2	2.4	2.6	2.8	3.0	3.2	3.4	3.6	3.8	4.0	4.2	4.4
											μ or np				
0	0.165	0.150	0.135	0.111	0.091	0.074	0.061	0.050	0.041	0.033	0.027	0.022	0.018	0.015	0.012
1	0.463	0.434	0.406	0.355	0.308	0.267	0.231	0.199	0.171	0.147	0.126	0.107	0.092	0.078	0.066
2	0.731	0.704	0.677	0.623	0.570	0.518	0.469	0.423	0.380	0.340	0.303	0.269	0.238	0.210	0.185
3	0.891	0.875	0.857	0.819	0.779	0.736	0.692	0.647	0.603	0.558	0.515	0.473	0.433	0.395	0.359
4	0.964	0.956	0.947	0.928	0.904	0.877	0.848	0.815	0.781	0.744	0.706	0.668	0.629	0.590	0.551
5	0.990	0.987	0.983	0.975	0.964	0.951	0.935	0.916	0.895	0.871	0.844	0.816	0.785	0.753	0.720
6	0.997	0.997	0.995	0.993	0.988	0.983	0.976	0.966	0.955	0.942	0.927	0.909	0.889	0.867	0.844
7	0.999	0.999	0.999	0.998	0.997	0.995	0.992	0.988	0.983	0.977	0.969	0.960	0.949	0.936	0.921
8	1.000	1.000	1.000	1.000	0.999	0.999	0.998	0.996	0.994	0.992	0.988	0.984	0.979	0.972	0.964
9					1.000	1.000	0.999	0.999	0.998	0.997	0.996	0.994	0.992	0.989	0.985
10							1.000	1.000	1.000	0.999	0.999	0.998	0.997	0.996	0.994
11										1.000	1.000	0.999	0.999	0.999	0.998
12												1.000	1.000	1.000	0.959
13															1.000

c or r	μ or np														
	4.6	4.8	5.0	5.2	5.4	5.6	5.8	6.0	6.2	6.4	6.6	6.8	7.0	7.2	7.4
0	0.010	0.008	0.007	0.006	0.005	0.004	0.003	0.002	0.002	0.002	0.001	0.001	0.001	0.001	0.001
1	0.056	0.048	0.040	0.034	0.029	0.024	0.021	0.017	0.015	0.012	0.010	0.009	0.007	0.006	0.005
2	0.163	0.143	0.125	0.109	0.095	0.082	0.072	0.062	0.054	0.046	0.040	0.034	0.030	0.025	0.022
3	0.326	0.294	0.265	0.238	0.213	0.191	0.170	0.151	0.134	0.119	0.105	0.093	0.082	0.072	0.063
4	0.513	0.476	0.440	0.406	0.373	0.342	0.313	0.285	0.259	0.235	0.213	0.192	0.173	0.156	0.140
5	0.686	0.651	0.616	0.581	0.546	0.512	0.478	0.446	0.414	0.384	0.355	0.327	0.301	0.276	0.253
6	0.818	0.791	0.762	0.732	0.702	0.670	0.638	0.606	0.574	0.542	0.511	0.480	0.450	0.420	0.392
7	0.905	0.887	0.867	0.845	0.822	0.797	0.771	0.744	0.716	0.687	0.658	0.628	0.599	0.569	0.539
8	0.955	0.944	0.932	0.918	0.903	0.886	0.867	0.847	0.826	0.803	0.780	0.755	0.729	0.703	0.676
9	0.980	0.975	0.968	0.960	0.951	0.941	0.929	0.916	0.902	0.886	0.869	0.850	0.830	0.810	0.788
10	0.992	0.990	0.986	0.982	0.977	0.972	0.965	0.957	0.949	0.939	0.927	0.915	0.901	0.887	0.871
11	0.997	0.996	0.995	0.993	0.990	0.988	0.984	0.980	0.975	0.969	0.963	0.955	0.947	0.937	0.926
12	0.999	0.999	0.998	0.997	0.996	0.995	0.993	0.991	0.989	0.986	0.982	0.978	0.973	0.967	0.961
13	1.000	1.000	0.999	0.999	0.999	0.998	0.997	0.996	0.995	0.994	0.992	0.990	0.987	0.984	0.980
14			1.000	1.000	1.000	0.999	0.999	0.999	0.998	0.997	0.997	0.996	0.994	0.993	0.991
15						1.000	1.000	0.999	0.999	0.999	0.999	0.998	0.998	0.997	0.996
16								1.000	1.000	1.000	0.999	0.999	0.999	0.999	0.998
17											1.000	1.000	1.000	0.999	0.999
18														1.000	1.000

SELECTED VALUES OF THE POISSON CUMULATIVE DISTRIBUTION[a] (cont.)

c or r	7.6	7.8	8.0	8.5	9.0	9.5	10.0	10.5	11.0	11.5	12.0	12.5	13.0	13.5	14.0
							μ or np								
0	0.001	0.000	0.000	0.000	0.000	0.000	0.000	0.000	0.000	0.000	0.000	0.000	0.000	0.000	0.000
1	0.004	0.004	0.003	0.002	0.001	0.001	0.000	0.000	0.000	0.000	0.000	0.000	0.000	0.000	0.000
2	0.019	0.016	0.014	0.009	0.006	0.004	0.003	0.002	0.001	0.001	0.001	0.000	0.000	0.000	0.000
3	0.055	0.048	0.042	0.030	0.021	0.015	0.010	0.007	0.005	0.003	0.002	0.002	0.001	0.001	0.000
4	0.125	0.112	0.100	0.074	0.055	0.040	0.029	0.021	0.015	0.011	0.008	0.005	0.004	0.003	0.002
5	0.231	0.210	0.191	0.150	0.116	0.089	0.067	0.050	0.038	0.028	0.020	0.015	0.011	0.008	0.006
6	0.365	0.338	0.313	0.256	0.207	0.165	0.130	0.102	0.079	0.060	0.046	0.035	0.026	0.019	0.014
7	0.510	0.481	0.453	0.386	0.324	0.269	0.220	0.179	0.143	0.114	0.090	0.070	0.054	0.041	0.032
8	0.648	0.620	0.593	0.523	0.456	0.392	0.333	0.279	0.232	0.191	0.155	0.125	0.100	0.079	0.062
9	0.765	0.741	0.717	0.653	0.587	0.522	0.458	0.379	0.341	0.289	0.242	0.202	0.166	0.135	0.109
10	0.854	0.835	0.816	0.763	0.706	0.645	0.583	0.521	0.460	0.402	0.347	0.297	0.252	0.211	0.176
11	0.915	0.902	0.888	0.849	0.803	0.752	0.697	0.639	0.579	0.520	0.462	0.406	0.353	0.304	0.260
12	0.954	0.945	0.936	0.909	0.876	0.836	0.792	0.742	0.689	0.633	0.576	0.519	0.463	0.409	0.358
13	0.976	0.971	0.966	0.949	0.926	0.898	0.864	0.825	0.781	0.733	0.682	0.628	0.573	0.518	0.464
14	0.989	0.986	0.983	0.973	0.959	0.940	0.917	0.888	0.854	0.815	0.772	0.725	0.675	0.623	0.570
15	0.995	0.993	0.992	0.986	0.978	0.967	0.951	0.932	0.907	0.878	0.844	0.806	0.764	0.718	0.669
16	0.998	0.997	0.996	0.993	0.989	0.982	0.973	0.960	0.944	0.924	0.899	0.869	0.835	0.798	0.756
17	0.999	0.999	0.998	0.997	0.995	0.991	0.986	0.978	0.968	0.954	0.937	0.916	0.890	0.861	0.827
18	1.000	1.000	0.999	0.999	0.998	0.996	0.993	0.988	0.982	0.974	0.963	0.948	0.930	0.908	0.883
19			1.000	0.999	0.999	0.998	0.997	0.994	0.991	0.986	0.979	0.969	0.957	0.942	0.923
20				1.000	1.000	0.999	0.998	0.997	0.995	0.992	0.988	0.983	0.975	0.965	0.952
21						1.000	0.999	0.999	0.998	0.996	0.994	0.991	0.986	0.980	0.971
22							1.000	0.999	0.999	0.998	0.997	0.995	0.992	0.989	0.983
23								1.000	1.000	0.999	0.999	0.998	0.996	0.994	0.991
24										1.000	0.999	0.999	0.998	0.997	0.995
25											1.000	0.999	0.999	0.998	0.997
26												1.000	1.000	0.999	0.999
27														1.000	0.999
28															1.000

229

SELECTED VALUES OF THE POISSON CUMULATIVE DISTRIBUTION[a] (cont.)

c or r	μ or np											
	14.5	15.0	16	17	18	19	20	21	22	23	24	25
3	0.000	0.000	0.000	0.000	0.000	0.000	0.000	0.000	0.000	0.000	0.000	0.000
4	0.001	0.001	0.000	0.000	0.000	0.000	0.000	0.000	0.000	0.000	0.000	0.000
5	0.004	0.003	0.001	0.001	0.000	0.000	0.000	0.000	0.000	0.000	0.000	0.000
6	0.010	0.008	0.004	0.002	0.001	0.001	0.000	0.000	0.000	0.000	0.000	0.000
7	0.024	0.018	0.010	0.005	0.003	0.002	0.001	0.000	0.000	0.000	0.000	0.000
8	0.048	0.037	0.022	0.013	0.007	0.004	0.002	0.001	0.001	0.000	0.000	0.000
9	0.088	0.070	0.043	0.026	0.015	0.009	0.005	0.003	0.002	0.001	0.000	0.000
10	0.145	0.118	0.077	0.049	0.030	0.018	0.011	0.006	0.004	0.002	0.001	0.001
11	0.220	0.185	0.127	0.085	0.055	0.035	0.021	0.013	0.008	0.004	0.003	0.001
12	0.311	0.268	0.193	0.135	0.092	0.061	0.039	0.025	0.015	0.009	0.005	0.003
13	0.413	0.363	0.275	0.201	0.143	0.098	0.066	0.043	0.028	0.017	0.011	0.006
14	0.518	0.466	0.368	0.281	0.208	0.150	0.105	0.072	0.048	0.031	0.020	0.012
15	0.619	0.568	0.467	0.371	0.287	0.215	0.157	0.111	0.077	0.052	0.034	0.022
16	0.711	0.664	0.566	0.468	0.375	0.292	0.221	0.163	0.117	0.082	0.056	0.038
17	0.790	0.749	0.659	0.564	0.469	0.378	0.297	0.227	0.169	0.123	0.087	0.060
18	0.853	0.819	0.742	0.655	0.562	0.469	0.381	0.302	0.232	0.175	0.128	0.092
19	0.901	0.875	0.812	0.736	0.651	0.561	0.470	0.384	0.306	0.238	0.180	0.134
20	0.936	0.917	0.868	0.805	0.731	0.647	0.559	0.471	0.387	0.310	0.243	0.185
21	0.960	0.947	0.911	0.861	0.799	0.725	0.644	0.558	0.472	0.389	0.314	0.247
22	0.976	0.967	0.942	0.905	0.855	0.793	0.721	0.640	0.556	0.472	0.392	0.318
23	0.986	0.981	0.963	0.937	0.899	0.849	0.787	0.716	0.637	0.555	0.473	0.394
24	0.992	0.989	0.978	0.959	0.932	0.893	0.843	0.782	0.712	0.635	0.554	0.473
25	0.996	0.994	0.987	0.975	0.955	0.927	0.888	0.838	0.777	0.708	0.632	0.553
26	0.998	0.997	0.993	0.985	0.972	0.951	0.922	0.883	0.832	0.772	0.704	0.629
27	0.999	0.998	0.996	0.991	0.983	0.969	0.948	0.917	0.877	0.827	0.768	0.700
28	0.999	0.999	0.998	0.995	0.990	0.980	0.966	0.944	0.913	0.873	0.823	0.763
29	1.000	1.000	0.999	0.997	0.994	0.988	0.978	0.963	0.940	0.908	0.868	0.818
30			0.999	0.999	0.997	0.993	0.987	0.976	0.959	0.936	0.904	0.863
31			1.000	0.999	0.998	0.996	0.992	0.985	0.973	0.956	0.932	0.900
32				1.000	0.999	0.998	0.995	0.991	0.983	0.971	0.953	0.929
33					1.000	0.999	0.997	0.994	0.989	0.981	0.969	0.950
34						0.999	0.999	0.997	0.994	0.988	0.979	0.966
35						1.000	0.999	0.998	0.996	0.993	0.987	0.978
36							1.000	0.999	0.998	0.996	0.992	0.985
37								0.999	0.999	0.997	0.995	0.991
38								1.000	0.999	0.999	0.997	0.994
39									1.000	0.999	0.998	0.997
40										1.000	0.999	0.998
41											0.999	0.999
42											1.000	0.999
43												1.000

INDEX